Into the Heart of the Father

of the Father

Learning from and Giving
Yourself through Christ in Prayer

LEONARD J. DELORENZO

Blessings, Tim!

the WORD
among us®
press

Published by The Word Among Us Press
7115 Guilford Drive, Suite 100
Frederick, Maryland 21704
wau.org

25 24 23 22 21   1 2 3 4 5

ISBN: 978-1-59325-552-7
eISBN: 978-1-59325-553-4

Cover design by Suzanne Earl
Cover Art: Epaminonda, "The Prodigal Son,"
from the Sacred Art Pilgrim Collection (http://sacredartpilgrim.com).

Made and printed in the United States of America

Library of Congress Control Number: 2021904117

To my daughter Siena Elisabeth,
who was placed in my arms and I began to pray.

Contents

Let us begin our journey into prayer with a prayer:

I give you thanks, O LORD, with my whole heart;
    before the angels I sing your praise;
I bow down toward your holy temple
    and give thanks to your name for your mercy and your
faithfulness;
for you have exalted above everything
    your name and your word.
On the day I called, you answered me,
    my strength of soul you increased. . . .

. . . The LORD will fulfil his purpose for me;
    your mercy, O LORD, endures for ever. (Psalm 138:1-3, 8)

CHAPTER ONE

The Boundaries
of Prayer

The love of Christ sets the boundaries of Christian prayer.
Prayer is possible from any condition that Christ's love
reaches. That is because Christian prayer is nothing other and
nothing less than entering into Christ. We pray into Christ.

When Christians pray, we join in Christ's prayer. His prayer
is the only prayer: the prayer of the Son to the Father. From
his Father, Christ receives everything; and to his Father, Christ
gives everything. His prayer is the source of all love, and outside that love we do not have a prayer.

- By the incarnation, the Son of God has received the
  Father's love in the humanity he shares with us.
- By his passion and death, he has offered everything back
  to the Father through this same humanity.

- By his resurrection and ascension, Christ's humanity is raised up into his eternal union with his Father in the Spirit.

The beginning of prayer is the Son of God's descent to us, and the end of prayer is our ascent with him into the heart of the Father.

From where we are in our ordinary lives, it is hard to imagine what it would mean to be drawn into the heart of the Father. For me a memory—or maybe it is a collection of memories— illustrates this better than a million vague daydreams. You see, I used to love to jump into my father's arms. I would climb to the top of the tall spiral staircase in my childhood home, squeeze through the railings, and then yell, "Daddy, catch me!" as my father waited below to receive my flailing body. Then I would run back up the staircase and do it again. And again. And again and again and again.

I loved jumping into my father's arms so much that I would sometimes wait on the top of the staircase for him to come walking by, then, without warning, jump down yelling, "Daddy, catch me!" This was unwise, but even in his surprise and likely at the expense of his lower back, my father always caught me.

My own children seem to have inherited this proclivity, albeit without the aid of a very tall staircase to begin their descent. They make do with standing on the couch to jump onto me as I lie on the floor, or from the bedside table as I lie in bed. Or they will run at full sprint across the room as I walk in the door and hurl themselves up toward my arms, whether or not I am ready.

I have discovered something my father must have felt all those years ago: you're always ready to catch your child, even when you don't think you're ready.

From reflecting on these games of children, I have discovered something else: I could always jump into my father's arms because I already had a place in his heart. That memory of flying through the air from the top of the spiral staircase—a memory I can still *feel*—has come to be a metaphor of something deeper. I could lunge to my father from any height because I knew he would catch me. Just so, I could reach up from any low point because I knew he would lift me up. The same goes for my children and my heart.

Christ, the Beginning and End of Prayer

This memory of emerging from and going back into my father's arms helps me imagine what I have learned about prayer. That is, the descent and ascent of the Son of God is the movement of divine love that makes prayer possible. From the depths to which he plunges and the heights to which he reaches, those whom he claims as his own may pray. Christ's gift makes prayer possible, but his disciples' responsibility is to respond to this gift. Discipleship is born of prayer.

If discipleship requires prayer, the urgent question for each of us might well be *How do I pray?* In the pages that follow, I respond to that question but not in a manual-like, how-to fashion. Instead we will learn more about "how to pray" by placing the person of Christ at the center of our search and discovering how we may join in his prayer. This means that we will meditate on how far the love of Christ goes so that we might be drawn into that love with all that we have and all that we are. Ours is a search for the boundaries of Christ's love, in which we find the gift and responsibility of prayer.

Jesus prayed. He prayed human prayers. He prayed as a child, and he prayed as an adult. He prayed in sorrow, and he prayed in joy. He prayed in lament, and he prayed in thanksgiving. He listened, and he spoke. He heeded the Father, and he pleaded with the Father. Through it all, praying is not something he merely did; he is his prayer. Everything about Jesus says, "Dear Father."[1]

The Christian at prayer never prays alone. She prays in Christ, and Christ prays in her. Left to ourselves, we do not know how to pray. Christ teaches us how to pray, and moreover, Christ is himself the lesson. In him our lives come to say, "Dear Father."

In Christ we learn how to listen and how to speak—how to receive the will of our Father in heaven and how to act on it. We learn how to beg. We learn how to give thanks. We learn how to become fully human—to become his disciples and even his saints.

To know how to pray as Christians, we must know Christ; and to know Christ for who he is, we must know Scripture. As St. Jerome said, "Ignorance of Scripture is ignorance of Christ." Familiarity with Scripture leads to familiarity with Christ. Even more, growing in love of Scripture helps us grow in love of Christ.

In the end, "knowing Christ" is not strictly about knowledge; it is rather about love.[2] To know Christ means to love Christ and even to know ourselves as being loved by him. Scripture is the introduction to Christ that we never exhaust in this life.

All of Scripture testifies to "the Word [who] became flesh and dwelt among us" (John 1:14). In and through Scripture, we discover the height, depth, and breadth of God's love for the world in his only begotten Son (see John 3:16). But you could read Scripture over and over again without ever encountering the Word of God.

To encounter the Word of God, we must be available for the encounter. He is not a static word; rather the Word of God is personal. Christ offers himself fully to his Church. Within the Church, we are the ones called to receive him. The Word of God speaks to *us* in Scripture *if we have "ears to hear"* (Matthew 11:15; see Revelation 2:29). Christ will teach us how to hear better and how to hear more, but we must approach him with a willingness to listen. This is the humility from which discipleship emerges; it is how prayer begins.

Even the humility at the beginning of prayer is a gift. Christ sends us the Holy Spirit to bring us into his own humility. Christ is the one "who, though he was in the form of God, did not count equality with God a thing to be grasped, but emptied himself" (Philippians 2:6-7). When the Spirit "intercedes for us with sighs too deep for words," we come to share in Christ's humility: we are "conformed to the image of [the Father's] Son" (Romans 8:26, 29). We become beggars, more like a sinful tax collector than a puffed-up Pharisee, for "the LORD is near to the brokenhearted" (Psalm 34:18).[3]

The Journey Ahead

Together let us seek to rediscover who Christ is, how far his love goes, and how we are to pray. Approaching Scripture and principally the Gospels, we will try to let go of our stuffy assumptions in order to humbly listen. This requires trust, however, and I have lost much of the unadulterated capacity to trust that I felt when I threw myself into the arms of my father. Perhaps you are like me in this regard. I guard many things. I hold back. I tend to go it alone. I hesitate.

This reluctance and trepidation are nowhere more apparent than in the life of prayer. All too often, prayer becomes perfunctory, restrained, and even impersonal. Rarely is my prayer an exercise of giving my whole self to *someone*, entrusting to *him* all my cares and joys. It is more common to play it safe from the heights, to muddle through from the depths, than to lunge from wherever I am into the arms of the God who holds me in his heart.

And yet we hope to pray into Christ, who himself prayed and whose whole life was a prayer to the Father, a prayer without ceasing. The *Catechism of the Catholic Church* makes the path clear:

> To seek to understand [Christ's] prayer through what his witnesses proclaim to us in the Gospel is to approach the holy Lord Jesus as Moses approached the burning bush: first to contemplate him in prayer, then to hear how he teaches us to pray, in order to know how he hears our prayer. (*Catechism* 2598)

Those three steps set the itinerary for our journey into Christ's prayer: contemplate him, heed his lessons, and discover how he hears our prayer. This is all about the boundaries of prayer: how far, how to navigate, and how we change.

Contemplate Him in Prayer

First we will contemplate Christ in prayer. We will ponder Jesus at prayer, as presented to us through the Gospels. Jesus' prayer is a mystery, because his very human prayers are the eternal dialogue of the only begotten Son with his Father. We cannot approach these episodes of prayer as if they were merely interesting case studies where we might learn novel spiritual techniques for praying. Instead, as the *Catechism* attests, we must "contemplate him in prayer."

A "temple" is a space set aside for worship, so to "*con*-template" means to approach and gaze at something or someone "with" this kind of space set aside. Where does the one who contemplates set aside such a space? Within himself or herself. That means that we, as the ones who go to see Christ at prayer, must bring with us a willingness to wonder, to be surprised, and indeed to revere and adore the one at whom we gaze. All of that happens as much with our hearts as it does with our eyes and ears.

Contemplating Jesus is an act of faith seeking understanding because it begins with the confession that he is "the Christ, the Son of the living God" (Matthew 16:16). He is fully human and fully divine, so contemplating him at prayer requires us to praise the mystery of God-with-us. In him the Word of God is wedded to our humanity.

Yes, Jesus' prayers are human prayers, but this is not something to regret, as if his humanity were a thing to leave behind. Rather his humanity is the permanent sign and instrument for our union with God.[4] The Son came down from heaven to take on this humanity; and when he returned to heaven, he brought with him the humanity he had assumed.

The theologian Hans Urs von Balthasar touches on the mystery of the incarnation, to which all of Scripture directs us:

> Contemplation's ladder, reaching up to heaven, begins with the word of scripture, and whatever rung we are on, we are never beyond this hearing of the word. In contemplation, just as we can never leave the Lord's humanity behind us, neither can we get "beyond" the word in its human form. It is in the humanity that we find God, in the world of sense that we find the Spirit.[5]

The first step of our journey into Christ's prayer is to attend lovingly to what Scripture presents about Jesus' own prayer. In doing so, we will see how far the love of Christ goes.

Hear How He Teaches Us to Pray

When Jesus taught on the seashore or on the road, when he preached from the plain or on the mount, air filled the space between his mouth and his listeners' ears. This air was the medium through which his voice traveled. As air was then, so Scripture is now. From him to us, Scripture is the medium of his voice.[6]

Just as the air did not possess a sacred quality on its own, so the bare words we might find on any page of the Bible are no more than ordinary words. They are words in our human languages, the same words we use elsewhere for other purposes. What makes these words sacred is that the Word who was in the beginning with God, who was and is God, empties himself into these human words to speak to his Church. He speaks to us.

The important thing for those who gathered on the seashore and the roadside, on the plain and on the mount, was that they received and responded to the voice of the Lord, which passed through the air to reach their ears. What mattered was allowing his voice to enter into their hearts. So too with us.

When Jesus teaches people to pray, we are not merely listening in as he teaches other people. As the *Catechism* puts it, we are to "hear how he teaches *us* to pray" (2598, emphasis mine). His disciples asked him to teach them how to pray because they did not know how. If we are willing to ask him, we will hear the instruction that passed through the air between him and them as the very same instruction given to us through the testimony of Scripture. Each one of us becomes a recipient of his sermons, his parables, and his lessons.

So the second step of our journey into Christ's prayer is to attend studiously to what Jesus teaches about prayer in the Gospels. In doing so, we will learn from the Master how to join in his prayer to the Father.

Know How He Hears Our Prayer

Before we can know *how* he hears our prayer, we might want to know that he does in fact hear our prayer. The fact that our prayers matter to the one who "was in the form of God" (Philippians 2:6) is an inexhaustible mystery. Indeed, that our prayers matter to the Almighty says something significant about us, but it says more about him. His humility is the basis of our power in prayer.

We never stop contemplating Christ, even as we consider our own prayer. In continuing to contemplate him, we discover first *that* he hears our prayers and then *how* he hears them. He allows himself to be moved. He listens and responds. He gathers up and offers our prayers in his prayer to the Father. This says something significant about him, but he allows it to also say something significant about us. The power of our prayer is the fruit of his humility.

Christ makes our prayers his own as we offer our prayers in his name. He draws us into his communion with the Father as he mingles our words with his. We become what he is when we allow his voice to enter into us and our voices to echo in his. This is all a matter of the heart: our hearts become like his, whose heart holds all whom he claims as his own within the love of his Father.

This third and final step of our journey into Christ's prayer is a discovery of what it means to be a disciple. We come to this by studying and wondering at what it means to allow Christ to hear us. That he hears us is a gift, as is the manner in which he hears us. But giving our voices over to him in prayer is our responsibility of discipleship.

Into the Heart of the Father

There is no map that will show us how to become who we are created to be. Christ himself is the way. His prayer is not something he does; it is who he is. And for those who seek the fullness of life in him, his prayer is meant to change who we are. We become one in his prayer.

From beginning to end, our journey into the prayer of Christ must itself be a prayer. "No one comes to the Father, but by me," Jesus says (John 14:6). But he also says, "No one can come to me unless the Father who sent me draws him," and, "You did not choose me, but I chose you." (John 6:44; 15:16). To seek him means that he has already found us and drawn us to himself.

We cannot pray on our own. We are *given* a Father in heaven. We are *taught* how to entrust ourselves to him. We begin as his creatures, but we *become* his children in Christ. Christ is the one who always jumps, always reaches, always hastens to the arms of his Father. Christ makes a place for us in his Father's heart, so that we might give ourselves to the one who loves us wherever we are.

I did not think of prayer when I jumped from the staircase as a child. I just jumped. So too, the point of thinking about prayer is not to keep thinking about prayer when we pray; instead the point is to jump.

I was blessed with a good father who not only caught my little body all those years ago but has been ready to catch me throughout my life. Not everyone is equally blessed. But to each of us Christ gives his Father as *our* Father, so that we might come to rest where Christ himself is at home. If we enter into and remain in Christ, he will draw us into the heart of the Father.

For Reflection

1. Would you say that you have encountered the living Word of God in the Bible? If so, in what ways? If not, have you asked the Holy Spirit to lead and guide you as you read? Would you be willing to spend more time with Scripture and give more attention to it, maybe even with someone's help and guidance?

2. Consider your ability to trust God—to leap into the arms of the Father. What memories or experiences do you have that can help you picture or imagine what this might be like? Conversely, are there experiences that have diminished your ability to trust? What steps can you take to move toward greater trust in God's love for you?

3. We do not pray alone, even though we often pray privately. What does it mean to you that you never pray alone? How do you pray with and into Christ? How does he make his presence known to you?

Chapter Two

Contemplating Christ in Prayer: The Descent

Atop a mountain, Jesus was transfigured before Peter, James, and John. His face shone like the sun, and his garments became dazzlingly white. At these heights, the disciples saw Jesus as the fulfilment of the Law and the prophets, with Moses standing on one side of him and Elijah on the other.

Back down the mountain, Jesus healed a boy possessed of an unclean spirit. He drew near to suffering and with authority both rebuked and drove out what was opposed to God. He plunged into the world's misery to restore what had been lost.

The disciples ascended with Jesus to witness his union with God, and they descended with Jesus to witness his union with us. In between the ascent and descent, the disciples received a simple and direct command. They heard the Father on high tell them to "listen to him" (Mark 9:7). What matters is not simply to "listen to what he says" but—like Peter, James, and John—to "listen to *him*." To do so is to follow the Father's instruction.

In our desire to learn how to pray, it is tempting to rush to analyze Christ's words, diagram his postures, or memorize his lessons. But the education of a disciple is first of all about gazing upon Christ himself, being ready and willing to follow where he leads, marveling at what he does, and hearing what he says.

The Father beseeches us to tune our eyes and ears, our minds and our hearts, to his beloved Son in a way unlike the way we attend to others. What was true for those three disciples is true for us: contemplating him means being willing to pitch our tent with him, to dwell with him, and to set out again and again to follow him. This requires an openness and readiness to be with him, as tentative and uncertain as our openness and readiness may be. He will begin to reveal to us the height, depth, and breadth of his love if we are willing to see him for who he is (see Romans 8:39). This is what it means to contemplate him in prayer: to enter into his union with the Father and welcome his communion with us.

"Listen to him," the Father says (Mark 9:7), and so we shall. Throughout this chapter, we will listen to him who descends to the womb of the Virgin, into the waters of the Jordan, and beneath the world in the darkness of the tomb. In the next chapter, we will keep listening to him who rises on the third day, who ascends to heaven, and who is seated at the right hand of the Father. Between the descent and the ascent, we will contemplate Christ in prayer as we "listen to him."

Descending, He Dwelt among Us

"The Word became flesh and dwelt among us" (John 1:14), and his name is Jesus. When Jesus speaks, he speaks with human words. When he acts, he acts with human actions. And when he prays, he prays as one of us: with human prayers. All of this increases rather than diminishes the oddness of that unforgettable line St. John wrote: "And the Word became flesh." What Jesus says, does, and prays manifests nothing less than the full mystery of God, because that is who he is: God-with-us.

Jesus is the humility of God. He who "was in the form of God . . . emptied himself" (Philippians 2:6, 7) to become one with us. This descent of God is the mystery of the incarnation—a mystery whose depth begins in the silence of the womb and sinks to the silence of the tomb. In Jesus the love of God goes to the very bottom.

God's loss is our gain in Christ. By his life, he takes on the full human condition. He even takes on our sin, though he is without sin. He goes to and beyond the limits of who and what we are so that he might offer everything back to the Father. That is his complete act of prayer: he comes down to gather us up into his Father's love.

This movement of Christ's descent to share in our condition is reflected in the lives of his saints. I find it especially resplendent in the witness of St. Damien of Molokai.

In 1865 the Hawaiian government began to permanently quarantine those who had or were suspected of having leprosy in a colony on the island of Molokai. These abandoned people cried out for priests and ministers to accompany them and tend to their spiritual needs. Fr. Damien was the first to go, and by his own request, he remained with these people for the rest of his life, even as he contracted leprosy. By his company and through his ministry, the abandoned and desolate people of this colony were not alone: they were raised up in love to God. St. Damien moved as the Son of God moved when he took flesh to dwell among us.

If we are to "listen to" Jesus, our first task is to contemplate his descent to us. How does he take on our condition? What does it look like and sound like when the Word of God prays human prayers? How far down does he go to gather us up?

Our joy begins in his sorrow, our life in his death.

Son of Mary

Jesus' prayer begins with Mary. Her yes to the Father's will reverberates through the conception of Jesus by the Holy Spirit, and it never ceases. The Word of God humbles himself before the words of his mother: her words are the first words in the life of Jesus.

The Word of God became flesh in the womb of the Virgin. The very body and blood that he offers for the life of the world are gifts that he first received (see Hebrews 10:5; Psalm 40:6-8). By his body and blood, Jesus says thank you. He is *eucharistia*. Balthasar ponders:

> Whom does he thank? Most certainly he thanks God the Father
> ... [but he also] thanks the poor Maid from whom he received
> this flesh and blood through the overshadowing of the Holy

Spirit. . . . [From her] he learns to say Yes, *fiat*. . . . This is the Catholic prayer that Jesus learned from his human mother.[7]

The humility of the Incarnate Word begins in his obedience to Mary. He receives from her, he is formed in her, he is taught by her. In the transfiguration, the Father will direct Jesus' disciples to "listen to him," yet Jesus humbles himself to listen to *her*.

Listening to Mary began in utero. This is not only a spiritual statement; it is indeed a biological statement. As we know from modern science, prenatal children develop the ability to hear at around sixteen to eighteen weeks of gestation. Moreover, as the physician and professor of internal medicine Dr. Kristin Collier states, "The ability of a baby to hear her mother's voice vibrating inside the uterus is one way in which bonding occurs," and "The mother's voice is reported to be the most intense acoustical signal measured in the amniotic environment."[8]

To heed this scientific fact in reference to the Incarnate Word in Mary's womb, we do well to ponder these words of Dr. Collier:

Consider when Mary sings to the LORD Jesus in her womb [at the Visitation]; we can only imagine that this was not the last time she sang to her Son who is our LORD. We can infer that baby Jesus was physiologically shaped by his mother's voice. This is a great mystery of our faith: that our incarnate LORD Jesus, the Word made flesh, the very voice of the LORD, the One through whom the world was formed, was himself physically shaped by his Mother Mary's voice on earth.[9]

Both theologically and physiologically, we are right to confess that the words of Mary reverberate in the body and blood of Jesus.

This mystery runs deeper still, as Dr. Collier again helps us recognize. As with every mother, the placenta within Mary's womb was a "fetomaternal organ because it [was] made by both the baby and mother (and Providence). The placenta is the only purposely transient organ in humans and is the only single organ created by two people in cooperation."[10] As a prenatal child, Jesus did not passively abide within his mother: he cooperated with her.

The exchange between mother and child does not end with the placenta though, nor does the exchange cease at birth, nor does the exchange only benefit the child. "We know that genetic material from the prenatal child crosses through the placenta and can be found in [the] mother's circulation."[11] These cells are not inert or lifeless but instead "become integrated into maternal tissue and are active and working in ways that we are just beginning to understand."[12]

This means that the Word made flesh remained in his mother's body on the cellular level, animating her physiologically even as he enlivened her spiritually. As Dr. Collier concludes, "We can say that Mary not only carried the Son of God in her body when he was in her womb, but that she likely carried his cells in her body throughout her life in a way that further magnifies her position as the glorious Theotokos."[13]

The first Eucharistic exchange is between Jesus and Mary. He who received his body and blood from her offers his thanks by abiding in her flesh and blood. She who was not

God shares in the life of God through the blessed fruit of her womb, Jesus.

The first marvelous thing in the prayer of Jesus is not what he prays for but what he prays *with*. The Word of God and only begotten Son of the Father prays *with* a human body, *with* human words, *with* human gestures—in sum, he prays *with* the humanity he received. Because Christ has taken on our humanity, our humanity becomes the site of prayer. This prayer begins in Mary.

Son of Israel

From his mother, Jesus did indeed receive "his flesh and his blood, his heartbeat, his gestures, his language," but he "also received forms of thinking and looking at things, all that was imprinted upon his human soul."[14] When the Word of God took on human flesh, he deigned to take on a particular history, a set of customs, and we might even say, a certain perspective on the world. He is a man with ancestors and a unique lineage, born into a specific time and place. He inherits what his forebears bequeathed to him.

This is not at all a foreign idea for us. All of us are the children of our parents and in some significant way inheritors of a past we did not live. This reality has inspired many great stage dramas. Consider the story of Romeo and Juliet, who were a Montague and a Capulet respectively, each inheriting all that their history meant. And in the musical *Hamilton*, we see Aaron Burr and Alexander Hamilton singing to their young children that their parents will fight and bleed for them *now* so that they, along with the nation, will have a strong foundation. "We'll pass it on to you," they sing, "we'll give the world to you."[15] Indeed, Philip Hamilton proved to be *too much* his father's son.

On a more prosaic level, when my wife Lisa and I were married, we brought our heritages together, just as every married couple does. That meant that a patient and kind woman raised in the South started to share a home and a life with a quick-witted and often sarcastic Italian American born in northern New Jersey. Many generations went into forming us as we were on our wedding day. We each receive and live our lives upon what our forebears bequeath to us.

We find in the genealogy with which St. Matthew opens his Gospel that Jesus' lineage runs back forty-two generations to Abraham, from whom the people of Israel emerged (see Matthew 1:1-17). Through his foster father Joseph—the husband of Mary—Jesus is united to and assumes the history of Israel as his own: beginning with the patriarchs, through the monarchy of David, into the exile at the hands of the Babylonians, and up to the household of Joseph, under whose name Jesus was enrolled with Mary by the decree of Caesar Augustus (Luke 2:1-6).

Under threat of persecution, Mary's husband, Joseph (son of Jacob), followed the path of his namesake Joseph (son of the patriarch Jacob) in flight to Egypt (see Matthew 2:13-15; Genesis 37:36; 46:1-26). Just as the whole house of Israel went down to Egypt under the protection of the patriarch Joseph in ages past, so does Jesus go down to Egypt under the protection of his father Joseph. What God speaks through

his prophet Hosea about the people of Israel is thereby fulfilled in Jesus:

> When [he] was a child, I loved him,
>   and out of Egypt I called my son. (Hosea 11:1)

This Jewish identity was marked on Jesus' flesh when, eight
days after his birth, he was circumcised in accordance with
the law of Israel, founded on the covenant with Abraham (see
Luke 2:21; Genesis 17:10-14). Through the fidelity of his parents, Jesus was presented in the Temple and placed in the arms
of the priest Simeon, who proclaimed the child as the long-
awaited anointed one (Luke 2:22-35). And again, under the
obedience and custom of Mary and Joseph, Jesus returned
to the Temple every year on pilgrimage; his obedience to his
parents was directed to his Father in heaven (Luke 2:41-52).

None of this is mere biography; rather it is the continuing humility of the divine descent. The only begotten Son of
God becomes a son of Israel: by lineage, by ritual, and by custom. He studies the Jewish Scriptures. He observes the Law of
Moses. He heeds the prophets. What began in the womb of
the Virgin continues in the people of Israel: the Word of God
receives the humanity he takes on from them. When he prays,
he prays not just *for* Israel but *with* Israel and indeed *as* Israel.
He prays in the words of Israel, with the memory of Israel,
according to the hope of Israel. He receives from Israel a tra-
dition, and he gives back to Israel his identity, making Israel
what it is called to be: the son of God (see Exodus 4:22; Psalm
2:7; Hosea 11:1).

Son of Adam, Son of Eve

On the threshold of his public ministry, Jesus stood on the banks of the River Jordan, waiting with ordinary sinners to go down in the murky waters under the hands of John the Baptist. John called sinners to repent, and those who flocked to him came because they recognized that they were in fact sinners. Jesus came with them, standing among them, waiting his turn. "Now when all the people were baptized, and when Jesus also had been baptized" (Luke 3:21): it sounds as if Jesus went last.

Why stand among sinners—even waiting behind them— to receive a baptism that they needed but he did not? Why be confused with them and humbled in their midst? Because when the Word became flesh, he sought to share everything with those whose flesh he received, including the condition of the sins for which they and not he were culpable. The Son of God went down into the water to join himself to sinners.

How far down would he go, this "beloved Son" with whom the Father is "well pleased" (Luke 3:22)? In the genealogy he provides in his Gospel, St. Luke lets us know: "Jesus, . . . being the son (as was supposed) of Joseph" (3:23) was united not only to the whole history of Israel, as "the son of Abraham" (3:34), but also to the firstborn of all creation as "the son of Adam, the son of God" (3:38). Under those waters, Jesus was united to the condition of Adam, under whose sin all humanity suffers. The Son of God assumed a place in the line of sinners who came forth from Adam, that he would be called one of the sons of Adam.

Even more, Jesus took his place as a son of Eve. Immediately after his baptism in the Jordan, through which he was united to the whole human race, "Jesus, full of the holy Spirit . . . was led by the Spirit for forty days in the wilderness, tempted by the devil" (Luke 4:1-2). The whole of those forty days was a temptation, but it culminated in three distinctive temptations.

The devil tempted Jesus by telling him to turn a stone into bread, by having him gaze upon all the kingdoms of the world, and by challenging him to wield his knowledge of God's word to his own advantage, to save himself and be praised (see Luke 4:3-12). These are the three ways of fallen desire that Eve instituted when she "saw that the tree was good for food, and that it was a delight to the eyes, and that the tree was to be desired to make one wise" (Genesis 3:6; see 1 John 2:16). Jesus, who was the beloved of the Father and full of the Spirit, went willingly into the desert to face the same temptations under which the mother of all the living fell. Why? To be united to her and all her offspring as a son of Eve.

The descent of the Son of God reaches back to the origins of the human race and its folly of original sin. The Word of God deigns to take on the flesh of humanity as it is, though he himself is without the sin that alienates the children of Adam and Eve from God. Jesus allows their voices to mingle in him. Thus when he prays, he prays not just *for* them but as one of them, in union with them, in them. The descending love of God breaks the seal of sin and, by way of Israel and without replacing Israel, reaches to all humanity.

Son of Sorrow

The descent of the Son of God does not leave him unaffected, as if he passed through the conditions of humanity with untroubled stoicism, protected by impenetrable armor. He suffered what others suffer: he chose to suffer for them and with them.

According to the Gospel of John, Jesus' first sign was performed at the wedding at Cana, where he allowed his mother's plea to move him. His final sign, according to the same Gospel, was the raising of his friend Lazarus. Just as at the wedding at Cana, where he allowed himself to be troubled before he acted with the power of God, in Bethany he sank into the grief and sorrow of those mourning Lazarus's death before he raised his friend from the tomb.

"When Jesus saw [Lazarus's sister Mary] weeping, and the Jews who came with her also weeping, he was deeply moved in spirit and troubled" (John 11:33). Moved and troubled, he did not shy away from the sorrow but asked to be brought closer to its source: "Where have you laid him?" (11:34). As he followed them to where the decomposing corpse of their beloved one was enclosed, he continued to open himself to the sorrow they suffered, even though he knew that the Father had entrusted him with power to give and restore life. When he arrived at the tomb, he yielded to their sorrow, taking it on as his own: "Jesus wept" (11:35). And before revealing the glory of God, he chose again to be "deeply moved" (11:38).

In the Letter to the Hebrews, we read, "Although he was a Son, he learned obedience through what he suffered" (5:8). His obedience was always preeminently to his Father in heaven, and in accordance with the Father's will, he was obedient to the conditions of our humanity. In Bethany that obedience meant sharing the sorrow of those cut off from their beloved by death.

Jesus does not merely hover above the moment of deep human connection when, for example, you cry with your best friend at her brother's funeral. He enters into communion with the sorrowful by allowing your sorrow to become his own sorrow—he feels it. Human sorrow is not foreign to Jesus: he can "sympathize with our weaknesses" (Hebrews 4:15).[16]

Son of Agony

Christ's sorrow is not merely the sorrow of men; his, uniquely, is the sorrow of God. He who is betrayed, condemned, and crucified bears in himself the pain of the world's rejection of God. Jesus is God's offer of love for the world, but the world preferred its own darkness to the light of his love (see John 3:16-19).

When Jesus enters into the Garden of Gethsemane as night approaches, he knows that his betrayer will be at hand. As his last act before he is bound by the might of others, Jesus prays. He prays with all the sorrow of the Almighty, so that in Christ, this divine sorrow becomes mental, spiritual, and physical anguish. Among men, Christ alone knows the depths of God's plaintive cry: "O my people, what have I done to you?" (Micah 6:3).

The love of God meets the world's lack of love in the body and blood of Jesus Christ. When he went down into the water of the River Jordan to join sinners in their condition, he allowed himself to become subject to the consequences of their sins, which he took on as if they were his own. Now, in the garden, he begins to realize the full weight of those sins in the world's rejection of God: "it was our pain that he bore" (Isaiah 53:4, NABRE).

The abandonment of his three closest disciples, who will not keep watch with him, is the nearest image of the abandonment that goes infinitely deeper. The odiousness and cruelty of it all is felt by Christ alone: "They hated me without a cause" (John 15:25, alluding to Psalm 35:19; 69:4). We cannot see the sorrow of God in the Garden of Gethsemane, nor can we know how God sees our sins. All we can see is Christ at prayer. His posture, his pleading, his sweat, and his tears: these are the objects of our contemplation. As we have said from the start, contemplation necessitates an openness to reverence, wonder, and adoration.[17]

Walking behind him into the garden as one of his disciples, we see him separate from the others to pray in solitude. St. Luke tells us that he "knelt down and prayed" (22:41), St. Mark that "he fell on the ground and prayed" (14:35). St. Matthew observes more still: "he fell on his face and prayed" (26:39). With his knees or even his face pressed to the earth, Jesus enters into prayer in a posture of submission, of humility, of lowliness. His prayer is as much bodily as it is mental or vocal. "Although he is the only Son of God, he assumes the uncomfortable position of any human being who prays."[18]

Jesus' descent from the Father has brought him here; his weight digs into the ground. With the humanity he received from us, he looks up to his Father in heaven to plead, "Father, if you are willing, remove this chalice from me" (Luke 22:42).

He finds no delight in the malice of others, in their hardness of heart, in their rejection of God through their rejection of him. This is a bitter drink, one that no one else could taste. He alone—who shares equality with God—can know and experience the sorrow of this fate. He is not untroubled, nor is he unmoved. As he tells his disciples, "My soul is very sorrowful, even to death" (Matthew 26:38).

To contemplate his posture and his pleading is to reach for the very mystery of God. This is the one through whom "all things were made" (John 1:3), and here he assumes the position and utters the words of one who cannot help himself. No human comes closer to their utter creaturely dependency than when he must rely completely on the help of another. Although not a creature, the only begotten Son of God willingly enters into that state of dependency: he places himself completely at the mercy of his Father. He begs.

"Nevertheless not my will, but yours, be done" (Luke 22:42). Here the mystery deepens. Jesus places his petition into his Father's hands. What he longs for with his body, his mind, his heart, and his soul, he yields to his greatest and final longing: the longing to be one with his Father and to do his Father's will. He holds back nothing from that ultimate prayer.

From his conception, Jesus was surrounded by the words of his mother: "let it be to me according to your word" (Luke 1:38). Those words resonate now in Mary's Son, who prays that same prayer to his Father. This is the prayer he teaches all who follow him: "Our Father, . . . thy will be done." In the garden, he prays what he teaches others to pray, what his Blessed Mother prayed at the moment he entered her womb.

Praying "more earnestly . . . his sweat became like great drops of blood falling down upon the ground" (Luke 22:44). Placing himself at the service of his Father's will does not relieve the tension of Jesus' prayer; rather the tension intensifies. Just as his humility is marked by his knees and face pressed to the ground, so the passion and the strain of his trial in prayer course through his veins and fall to the ground in his sweat, precious as blood. He entered the garden by his own power, but he knows that he will leave under the power of others. This is the path of his Father's will: to give himself completely to us.[19]

Placing himself in his Father's hands means placing himself in the hands of others. Whose hands are those? "The hands of sinners" (Mark 14:41). He gives himself into the hands of those who reject God, who wound God with their infidelity. Jesus gives himself willingly.

In his agony, the Son of God descends into the hands of those who love him not.[20]

Son of Man

The mission of Jesus' life was always to put himself into our hands. He did not seek death; he sought communion with us in obedience to his Father's will. That he would be handed over was never in doubt; how he would be received was the only question. He was spurned.

And yet his mission of communion did not cease as he was nailed to the cross. He turned that wood into the final instrument of communion. While suspended from those beams, he assumed the prayers of all mankind and offered them as his own prayer to his heavenly Father, giving his body and blood as the basis of our communion.

Christ's offering on the cross was the work of a lifetime. He prayed his way into this offering. During all those nights spent in solitude, praying to his Father, Jesus took as his own the words of the psalms. The psalms contain and express the entire human condition, from the deepest lament to the highest acclamation. Pressing our ear to Jesus on the cross, we hear the Word of God uttering our human prayers in an act of communion with his Father.

"My God, my God, why have you forsaken me?" (Matthew 27:46; Mark 15:34). How can these words that confess abandonment be words of communion? Because in Jesus' cry from the cross, he offers the very human words of Psalm 22:1.

Who among us has not felt all alone at some point in our life? As if even God has departed from us and our cries by day and night go unheeded? To join in union with all those who moan in this desperation, the Son of God experiences that loneliest loneliness and makes their prayer his own.

And by uttering the opening of this psalm of lament, Christ invokes the remainder of the psalm, in which God's deeds of liberation in days gone by are recalled, the present persecution is bemoaned, a fresh prayer for deliverance is uttered, and a final testament of faith in the fidelity of God is recited. Christ prays the whole of Psalm 22, from the opening condition of abandonment to the ultimate act of trust in God.

"Father, into your hands I commit my spirit!" (Luke 23:46). Here Christ speaks aloud the act of trust that is assumed but unspoken in his previous cry. These too are words from the psalmist: "Into your hand I commit my spirit" (Psalm 31:5). The one who prays these words is in distress but ready to offer thanksgiving for God's deliverance: "You have redeemed me, O LORD, faithful God." The psalm is a prayer of trust, suspended between the precarity of the present and the anticipation of God's coming salvation:

> In you, O LORD, I seek refuge; . . .
>   rescue me speedily! . . .
>
> I am in distress; . . .
>
>   . . . terror on every side! . . .
>
>   . . . save me in your merciful love! . . .
>
> O how abundant is your goodness,
>   which you have laid up for those who fear you,
>   and wrought for those who take refuge in you.
>   (Psalm 31:1, 2, 9, 13, 16, 19)

The beloved Son's trust in his Father undergoes trial on the cross, and yet trust he does, bearing the weight of rejection and throwing himself without reserve into the arms of his Father. He takes on the psalmist's whole prayer and fulfills it in himself.

"I thirst" (John 19:28). Jesus knew the hearts of his crucifiers. He knew that for his thirst they would give him vinegar to drink, as he would have prayed Psalm 69:21. Those who are drunk with ridicule (69:12), who insult the brokenhearted and give no comfort to the one in need of pity (69:20), do not respond with compassion to his thirst but make it worse.

Jesus cried out with thirst in communion with those whom St. Teresa of Calcutta named the "unwanted, unclaimed, unloved."[21] As the object of ridicule, he allowed his suffering to become a further source of ridicule: "They put a sponge full of . . . vinegar on hyssop and held it to his mouth" (John 19:29).

"When Jesus had received the vinegar, he said, 'It is finished'; and he bowed his head and gave up his spirit" (John 19:30). The mission was accomplished: he had put himself into our hands and withheld nothing. The cup that did not pass from him was the utter lack of compassion of those to whom he gave everything.

"Father, forgive them; for they know not what they do" (Luke 23:34).[22] What do "they" not know? They do not know that they play the part of the ones who persecute the innocent sufferer, and their offenses are counted as against God himself. For in the same verse, the evangelist reports that "they cast lots to divide his garments." This places them right in the midst of Psalm 22: "They divide my garments among them, and for my clothing they cast lots" (22:18). It is the psalm of him who cries out in abandonment and longs for God's deliverance (see 22:19).

Jesus alone knows what they are doing, and his knowledge is held within the passion of the psalm. And he who knows full well the immeasurability of the offense prays for forgiveness for those who commit it. In the very act by which the crucifiers reject God, the Son of God prays for forgiveness for them and offers himself as the bond of reconciliation.[23]

Christ prepared for this work of communion on the cross over his years and years of prayer. He who prayed the psalms anticipated and accepted as his mission the final rejection he would endure in obedience to his Father's will.

There is no part of the human condition absent from the 150 psalms. Christ prayed them all. In these prayers, he emptied himself and made his dwelling among us. The Incarnate Word offered these human words as his own prayer. He saw himself in these psalms, and he fulfilled the psalms in himself.

We catch a glimpse of what it means for Christ to take on the words of the psalms when we look at martyrs like the four churchwomen of El Salvador who were killed by government forces in December of 1980.[24] They had spent so much time and energy heeding the needs of the oppressed and mistreated persons of El Salvador that they spoke and thought and felt like the people they served. When they advocated for justice in the land, they did so in the language of those with whom they had shared life. They were killed, in fact, because of how closely they identified with and sounded like the poor of El Salvador. The condition of the people had become their condition.

We catch another glimpse when we look at Fr. Greg Boyle, SJ, who ministers to former and active gang members in Los Angeles. He has spent so much time embedded in their situation and learning their ways that he has become fluent in their lingo. He speaks to them on their terms, wrapping their words around his words so that the words mingle as one.[25]

To contemplate the prayer of Christ on the cross is to pray the psalms he prayed: the words he took as his own, the human condition to which he joined himself. In those words, Christ "prays for us, and prays in us, and is prayed to by us. . . . We must recognize our voices in him, and his accents in ourselves."[26] He who came into the world surrounded by Mary's voice breathed his last having taken on the voice of all humanity. By his descent, the Son of God became the Son of Man.

Son of Silence

"And [Joseph of Arimathea] bought a linen shroud, and taking him down, wrapped him in the linen shroud, and laid him in a tomb which had been hewn out of the rock; and he rolled a stone against the door of the tomb" (Mark 15:46). Lifeless, Jesus could not move himself, so Joseph took him down. Naked, he could not cover himself, so Joseph wrapped him in the shroud. Forsaken, this Son of Man had no place to lay his head, so Joseph laid him in the tomb.

When Joseph rolled the stone against the door, did that cut off Jesus' prayer? No, the silence was his prayer.

The silence of the dead is the end of the Son of God's descent among us. He reaches beyond the limits of speech to the endless stillness of those who are no longer. God called forth creation out of nothing, and by sin we, his beloved creatures, choose to return to the nothing from which we were called. In the last reckless plunge of the incarnation, the Word who was in the beginning with God, who was God, through whom all things were made, goes into the silence of those unmade by sin in death. "To there even Christ descended after his dying."[27]

Between the night of his crucifixion and the morning of his resurrection, Christ offers the silence of death as his prayer to his Father. Unlike his prayer in the garden, where we contemplate him in his posture and his words, or upon the cross, where his invocation of the psalms beckons us to contemplation, on Holy Saturday there is nothing to see, nothing to hear. It is precisely Jesus' absence of speech and lack of movement that we must contemplate.

He went to this depth to find us—all of us. "Listen to him."

To contemplate him in that tomb, where we cannot see him or hear him, means reckoning with the absolute limit of the possibility of prayer. Lying in solidarity with the solitary dead, Christ sets the boundary for the love of God. The psalmist asks,

> Where shall I go from your Spirit?
> Or where shall I flee from your presence? (Psalm 139:7)

Christ, who came from on high and descended below, answers, "Nowhere," because the love of God has gone everywhere in Christ. He offered in himself even the silence of our death to the Father, fulfilling what the psalmist prayed:

> If I ascend to heaven, you are there!
> If I make my bed in Sheol, you are there! (Psalm 139:8)

The descent to share all things with us, which began in the womb, is complete when Christ lies dead in the tomb. He assumed our words and our silence, our life and our death, in his single, unending prayer to the Father: "that they may all be one; even as you, Father, are in me, and I in you, that they also may be in us" (John 17:21).

For Reflection

1. Jesus cooperated with his mother even in utero, hearing her voice and sharing his life with her across the placenta they shared. Does the discussion in this chapter about the cooperation of Jesus and Mary through the fetomaternal placenta deepen your appreciation of Mary? How does this enrich your understanding of Mary as "Mother of God," who is also given to us as our own Blessed Mother?

2. Jesus stood shoulder to shoulder with sinners in baptism, not in judgment but in mercy. How willing are you to mingle with sinners in mercy, confident that God is present in their lives? Specifically, what have you done to accompany the needy on their journey?

3. God has gone to extraordinary lengths on behalf of humanity, descending into our dark world with his boundless love. What obstacles do you encounter to believing that he stands in solidarity with you? How can you let him "descend" into your life so that you may ascend with him into the joy that only God can give?

Chapter Three

Contemplating Christ in Prayer: The Ascent

Salvation comes in Christ alone, so whatever he does not assume as his own is not saved.[28] What part of the human condition has Christ failed to assume? In contemplating the descent of the Son of God, we have seen how he assumed everything from us, so that we might join in his communion with the Father. Will we?

In humility the Son of God descends to us in our lowliness, even to the point of becoming one with us in the death our sin brought about. He goes to the very bottom, not to remain there but that from beneath all he might raise us up to the height from which he came. Rising from the dead and ascending to the Father, he opens wide the path to our communion with God.

From any part of our human condition—in any state in which we find ourselves—we can raise our prayers to the Father because the Son of God has already assumed that part of our humanity in his divine love. He always prays that we "may all be one" in his communion with the Father (John 17:21). He makes our prayer possible, from the bottom up.

It can be hard to think about things from two directions at once, since we tend to cling to one perspective. When, for example, Pope Francis visited the United States in 2015, all the cameras on the tarmac captured the moment when he stepped out of his car to kiss Michael Keating—a ten-year-old boy in a wheelchair who suffers from severe cerebral palsy. The world marveled at the tenderness of Francis. What the world did not see was a movement from another direction: the life of the Keating family, which brought Michael to that kiss with Pope Francis.

It is a life of sacrifices made in love to care for Michael. The boy whom Pope Francis greeted is the same one who "feels the joy of his siblings' caresses," whom his family prays around and for, and who received his First Communion at St. Peter's Church in West Brandywine under the care of his pastor, Fr. Fitzpatrick.

"So many times we feel alone," Michael's mother said. "No one knows what we go through sometimes." The kiss from Pope Francis was a blessing to the whole Keating family, reaching all the hidden sacrifices and hardships and revealing them as holy.

The hidden life of the Keatings was being lifted up to God the whole time. The Holy Father encountered that life of love on the tarmac that day, for Michael is its gift and presence.[29]

St. Paul captures the unfathomable mystery of the descent and ascent of the Son of God in one breathtaking hymn of beauty and elegance. Christ comes from on high in eternal communion with the Father and descends below all creation, so that when he is raised and ascends back to the Father, all creation will be redeemed and glorified in him:

> Have this mind among yourselves, which was in Christ Jesus, who, though he was in the form of God, did not count equality with God a thing to be grasped, but emptied himself, taking the form of a servant, being born in the likeness of men. And being found in human form he humbled himself and became obedient unto death, even death on a cross. Therefore God has highly exalted him and bestowed on him the name which is above every name, that at the name of Jesus every knee should bow, in heaven and on earth and under the earth, and every tongue confess that Jesus Christ is Lord, to the glory of God the Father. (Philippians 2:5-11)

When the Father tells Jesus' disciples to "listen to him," he calls us to contemplate Christ in his descent *and* his ascent, as St. Paul grasps in faith. When he who "was in the form of God" humbled himself to become one with us, he turned everything he assumed from us into an offering to God. For us to accept that gift and allow our humanity to be taken up into that solemn offering, we must learn to give ourselves to him, as we truly are and just as we are.

In Christ we make our offering to the Father. This is what it means to pray: we pray in Christ, who turns our "mourning into dancing" and clothes us with his joy (Psalm 30:11).

Ascending, He Draws Us to the Father

The Word, who "became flesh and dwelt among us," rose from the dead on the third day (John 1:14). He rose still clinging to the flesh he had assumed from Mary, from Israel, from humanity. It is our flesh that is glorified in him. When he ascends to the right hand of the Father, that same human nature ascends in him, and his Blessed Mother follows, then all the saints.

The resurrection and ascension are the completion of the incarnation. The mystery of Christ is the whole movement: descending and ascending. Yes, Jesus is the humility of God, but the crucial thing is that *he is God*.[30] All the humbling and lowliness and suffering that we witness in the person of Jesus throughout his thirty-three years are chosen and endured by him as the one who was "in the form of God."

The first part of our contemplation according to Christ's descent had to do with his movement into communion with us. The second part, contemplating him according to his ascent, concerns his movement of our humanity into communion with his Father. Our prayer is in these two movements: receiving his communion with us and going with him into his communion with the Father.

Christ became what we are so that we might become what he is.[31] As St. Gregory of Nazianzus encourages us, "Let us seek to be like Christ, because Christ also became like us: to become [one with God] through him since he himself, through us, became a man. He took the worst upon himself to make us a gift of the best."[32] Contemplating his ascent from our lowliness to the glory of the Father, we discover how he makes us, in our humanity, into a gift.

He Who Is

"But who do you say that I am?" (Matthew 16:15; Mark 8:29; Luke 9:20). This is the decisive question of Christian discipleship. It elicits not so much a single response as an ongoing commitment. In saying, "You are the Christ, the Son of the living God" (Matthew 16:16), a disciple speaks not just with words but with the gift of his heart.

Jesus is the gift of God's love made personally present; he asks us to recognize him, receive him, and revere him for who he is. To "confess that Jesus Christ is Lord" (Philippians 2:11) is to say something fundamentally true about yourself—namely, that you are the one God loves and to whom God has given himself completely in Jesus Christ.

This is to be like the tax collector in Caravaggio's famous painting "The Calling of Saint Matthew." This man is seated at a table with others, counting the revenue he has taken from the people. From one side of the room comes Jesus, a ray of light following his gaze and his outstretched finger, all of which illuminate the tax collector's face.

The tax collector is stunned into recognition: he sees himself as the one at whom Jesus is looking. The light of Jesus' look of love has fallen on him before he has done anything to warrant it. What really matters at that moment is who is this Jesus who looks upon him?

By the movement of his heart, the tax collector accepts and responds to this look of love as more than a look from an ordinary person. His response shows that he has been caught in the look of divine love. And so it is that the tax collector leaves behind who he has been and becomes St. Matthew.[33]

To confess that Christ is Lord is only possible because God has made the first move: the Word became flesh and dwelt among us, and by that flesh he reveals himself as God to those called to him by faith. With ordinary eyes, we look upon this man; but by the eyes of faith, we see in this man "the glory of God the Father" (Philippians 2:11). He elevates our vision so that through him—by his flesh and blood—we may ascend to his heavenly Father (see 2 Corinthians 5:7).[34]

When Peter made his great confession of faith though, he immediately fell back down (see Matthew 16:22-23), just as, when walking on the water, he stopped gazing at Jesus in faith and immediately sank (14:30). On the sea, Peter had encountered the decisive question of discipleship in the midst of the storm, when Jesus walked towards him and said, "Take heart, it is I" (14:27). Jesus both speaks God's name—"I AM"[35]— and reveals himself as the one who holds power over the sea.[36]

The question is whether Peter will entrust himself to Jesus for who Jesus says he is and reveals himself to be. It is a question of Jesus' identity: "Lord, if it is you, bid me come to you on the water," and Jesus says, "Come" (Matthew 14:28, 29). When he trusts in Jesus as the power and wisdom of God, Peter walks on water by faith. But when he ceases to see and give himself to Jesus as the one who holds the wind and rain in his grasp, Peter sinks. It is stop-and-go with Peter when confronted with the decisive question of discipleship, the question of Jesus' identity.

Christ beckons us upward. The Son of God took on earthly things to draw us children of the earth to the heavenly things (see Colossians 3:2). In the muck and mire of the world, he who was "born in the likeness of men" (Philippians 2:7) is all too easy to overlook. He looks just like us—indeed, he *is* one of us. His very humanity hides the presence of God, yet it is through that humanity that God makes himself known.

Like Peter, all the disciples strained to see Jesus for who he is, seeing him indistinctly or in passing moments of faith-filled trust. Only by the light of the resurrection and the transformation of their hearts did the disciples begin to hold fast to the full mystery of Jesus. What was said of these disciples upon Jesus' entry into Jerusalem was true of them always: "His disciples did not understand . . . ; but when Jesus was glorified, then they remembered" (John 12:16; see also Mark 9:32; John 2:22).

Even Mary, who was without sin and heeded the Word of God without fail, pondered the mystery of her beloved Son (see Luke 1:29; 2:19, 51). When, according to the custom that Mary and Joseph passed on to him, Jesus went up to Jerusalem for Passover, Mary and Joseph confronted the upward movement that seeking Jesus requires. "And he said to them, 'How is it that you sought me? Did you not know that I must be in my Father's house?'" (2:49).

The evangelist then tells us that Joseph and Mary—even Mary, who is the paragon of discipleship and the only one whose faith in Jesus never wavers—"did not understand the saying which he spoke to them" (Luke 2:50). Why? Because understanding him and seeing him fully for who he is is never merely a matter of seeing him in the way that he comes to us. It is also a matter of following from the point where he meets us up to the heights from which he came: his Father's house.

Indeed Jesus, who knew himself to be the Son of the Father, "went down with them and came to Nazareth, and was obedient to them" (2:51). In other words, he went to dwell with and receive from Mary and Joseph all that they had and all that they were. By his obedience in their home, he fashioned them for obedience in his home with the Father. He came down to draw them up.

Unlike Peter, Mary did not stop gazing upon this child of hers with the eyes of faith. Rather she followed his lead and "kept all these things in her heart" (2:51). In the end, she who allowed the Son of God to make his home with her and assume everything from her was herself assumed into the home of her Son's heavenly Father.

"Let not your hearts be troubled; believe in God, believe also in me" (John 14:1). Mary's heart was troubled yet not by fear—rather by the pain of pondering Jesus ceaselessly in her heart and seeking him always.[37] Peter's heart, however, was troubled by fear and doubt. He gazed at the storm and not at Christ, and he sank (Matthew 14:30-31). He gazed at coming persecution and not at Christ, and he faltered (16:21-23). He gazed at his own peril and not at Christ, and he fell apart (26:69-75).

Both Mary and Peter confronted the awesome mystery of Jesus' identity, and both were tested in the heart. Mary sacrificed her heart to pondering Jesus always, while Peter went back and forth between trust and doubt in his heart. Mary followed Jesus unhesitatingly, while Peter had to be redeemed and rebuilt to seek after Jesus with all his heart.[38]

Whether by unfailing faith or by the resuscitation of faith through conversion, the question of discipleship is the same: "But who do you say that I am?" The answer is not given just in words but by following him back to where he came from—and following him there with all our hearts. Jesus is forthcoming in telling his disciples what he is about:

> In my Father's house are many rooms; if it were not so, would I have told you that I go to prepare a place for you? And when I go and prepare a place for you, I will come again and will take you to myself, that where I am you may be also. (John 14:2-3)

So who is he? The one who brings us home to the Father.

He Who Rises

"Did I not tell you that if you would believe you would see the glory of God?" (John 11:40). What the loved ones of Lazarus saw was Jesus drawing near to the source of their sorrow, to share in their sorrow and weep with them. And yet what would they eventually see? They would see more than they could as yet believe.

Outside Lazarus's tomb, Jesus raised his eyes to heaven (John 11:41). In his solitude, while looking toward his Father, he offered thanksgiving that his Father always hears him. Then he raised his voice and he commanded, "Lazarus, come out" (11:43).

The raising of his eyes and his voice and the offering of his prayer of thanksgiving all are proper to Jesus' human nature. He acted with his body, he spoke human words, and he uttered a human prayer. But those who remained with him at the tomb and heeded his command to roll away the stone, what then did they see? They saw "the dead man [come] out, his hands and feet bound with bandages, and his face wrapped with a cloth" (11:44). This indeed was the glory of God. Jesus raised the once-dead Lazarus by Jesus' divine nature.

Who was raised that day? Certainly Lazarus, for he with his inert and decaying flesh had no power to raise himself. But what about those who witnessed this sign? Did not they who had been gazing on this Jesus as he cloaked himself in their sorrow also see in him and through him the very glory of God?

"I am the resurrection and the life," he told Martha, "he who believes in me, though he die, yet shall he live, and whoever lives and believes in me shall never die. Do you believe this?" (John 11:25-26).

Many who witnessed his power came to believe not just in his work but in who Jesus is: the One whom the Father always hears and the one who raises everything to the Father. They could not see the eternal communion with his Father that was hidden in Jesus' prayer. All they could see was Jesus and the work her performed. By believing in him, they came to see the One who sent him. Out of their sorrow, Jesus lifted them to joy.

When Jesus walked into the Garden of Gethsemane some days later, three of his disciples saw him "sorrowful and troubled" (Matthew 26:37). Moving away from them, Jesus entered into his solemn prayer, pleading with his Father and offering to him his human will.

When Jesus came back to his disciples, he saw them asleep. He warned the disciples to pray so as not to succumb to temptation, yet their "flesh [was] weak" (26:41). As the disciples slept, Jesus made his trek alone.

In his human nature, Jesus underwent agony. He knelt and pressed his face to the ground, he sweated blood, and he uttered his prayers. By his divine nature, he carried his unbelieving, inattentive disciples into the communion he shared with his Father. His prayer—indeed his very body—was the instrument of lifting up this listless trio to the Father. Out of their slumber, they would be awakened to life in God.[39]

Jesus would go down into the grave to share in the lifelessness of humanity. It would not be the dead flesh of others that he would raise up in prayer. No, his own flesh lay in wait. At the bottom of his humanity was the apex of his divine power.

To undergo temptation, dishonor, crucifixion, and death, the Son of God emptied himself, allowing his divine nature to remain quiescent. Once in the grave with his human nature stilled, his share in the divine nature raised his body into everlasting glory. Jesus draws up with him to new life those whose death he humbled himself to share. In his resurrection, the prayers of all humanity for communion with the Father ascend. Out of the darkest night breaks the everlasting dawn.[40]

One such dark night was the one Fr. Maximillian Kolbe encountered at the end of his life. He was imprisoned in Auschwitz, maltreated and humiliated along with the other prisoners, seemingly rendered helpless. And yet Fr. Maximillian—who throughout his life had spent hours in Adoration before the Blessed Sacrament and had devoted himself to Mary, to hearing confessions, and to performing acts of self-sacrifice—persisted to the end in the light of God's love. In the darkness of Auschwitz, he became a light for others.

"He was like an angel to me," said Auschwitz survivor Simon Gershon. "Like a mother hen, he took me in his arms. He used to wipe away my tears. I believe in God more since that time."[41]

In the last wild gesture of his faith-filled life, St. Maximillian gave himself in place of a man condemned to death by starvation. The Catholic priest went into the starvation chamber with nine other men. In that dark and desolate place, he led his companions in prayer, comforted them, strengthened them, loved them. He was a light in the darkness, and the darkness did not overcome him. Christ's light dawned in Auschwitz.

What is the duty of those beckoned to believe in Christ's resurrection? The same duty that was given to Mary, to Peter, to Lazarus, and to St. Maximilian Kolbe: to listen to him. "Do not hold me," Jesus tells Mary Magdalene outside the tomb, "for I have not yet ascended . . . to my Father and your Father, to my God and your God" (John 20:17). The point of it all is to arise and go to the Father, who turns the night into day (see Amos 5:8).

He Who Ascends

"Simon Peter said to him, 'Lord, where are you going?' Jesus answered, 'Where I am going you cannot follow me now; but you shall follow afterward'" (John 13:36).

Jesus spoke these words to Peter before his passion and death. Afterward though—that is, *after* Jesus' passion, death, and resurrection—Jesus gave his final instruction to Peter: "Follow me" (John 21:19). In fact, Jesus said these words to Peter twice (see also 21:22). For Peter to follow Jesus would mean to follow into his passion and death, and Peter would eventually be crucified.

But even that obedient and sacrificial death was not the end of following Christ. When Jesus spoke to Peter about following him *afterward*, he did not present death as the end of the disciple's journey. *Afterward* meant *after* the passion and death—indeed, it meant *after* the resurrection and *after* Jesus ascended to the Father, "that where I am you may be also" (John 14:3). Not where Jesus *was* but where Jesus *is*, eternally: "in my Father's house" (14:2; see Luke 2:49).

How is it possible for Peter or any disciple to obey Jesus' command to "follow me" when the journey's end is his heavenly home? For Peter or for any of us, the journey is impossible on our own. It is only possible because, as Jesus promises, "I will come again and will take you to myself" (John 14:3). He will come to us from beyond our sight (Acts 1:9). He will come in glory, *still* clinging to the flesh he received in Mary's womb, the same flesh that was revealed in glory on the morning of the third day. He will come with *our* humanity to reveal *our* glory. He will come so we may see what we cannot see now, so we may be where we are not now, so we may become what we have not yet fully become. His coming again in glory at the end of time begins in our prayer today.

Christ's ascension is the seal of the incarnation. It is not just a movement up but the completion of union in heaven. In Mary's womb, the Word of God was united to human flesh; in Christ's ascension, that same flesh is given its final home in the communion of God.[42] The ascension did not just happen once, nor is it only coming in the future. For Christians, the ascension is happening now. Jean Corbon expresses this mystery beautifully:

> Jesus is, of course, at his Father's side. If, however, we reduce this "ascent" to a particular moment in our mortal history, we simply forget that beginning with the hour of his Cross and Resurrection Jesus and the human race are henceforth one. He became a son of man in order that we might become sons of God. The Ascension is progressive "until we all . . . form the perfect Man fully mature with the fullness of Christ himself" (Ephesians 4:13). The movement of the Ascension will be complete only when all the members of his body have been drawn to the Father and brought to life by his Spirit.[43]

Our humanity is brought into the intimate union of Christ with his Father through the gift of the Holy Spirit, who fell upon the apostles, forms the Church, and is imparted to every

Christian. Those of us who die to ourselves in the waters of Baptism, who are nourished at the Eucharistic table, and who are sealed with the Holy Spirit live no longer for ourselves or by ourselves, but as St. Paul says, "Christ . . . lives in me; and the life I now live in the flesh I live by faith in the Son of God" (Galatians 2:20). Christ's life becomes our life as he gives the source of his life to us: the Holy Spirit, who is the Son's communion with his Father.

The Spirit whom Christ gives to his disciples fills us with vital power, infusing us with the fire of love and freeing us to do great things, or rather small things with great love, as St. Thérèse of Lisieux and St. Teresa of Calcutta might put it. The Spirit imparts the true freedom and joy that set a person ablaze in charity, preferring nothing to serving others in God's name.

That is the story of St. Philip Neri. By his own testimony, given only to his most intimate companions, he received the Holy Spirit into his heart in a particularly powerful way one night while praying, as was his custom, in the dark catacombs of Rome.[44] This was the secret to his famous and unbounded joy: the Spirit of Christ lived within him.

This joy was intense and powerful, and its effects in the life of this great saint were remarkable. St. John Henry Newman proclaimed these marvels when telling of St. Philip's ministry of reconciliation:

> We are told in his Life, that "he abandoned every other care, and gave himself to hearing confessions." Not content with the day, he gave up a considerable portion of the night to it also.

Before dawn he had generally confessed a good number. When he retired to his room, he still confessed every one who came; though at prayers, though at meals, he broke off instantly, and attended to the call. When the church was opened at daybreak, he went down to the Confessional, and remained in it till noon, when he said Mass. When no penitents came, he remained near his Confessional; he never intermitted hearing confessions for any illness. "On the day of his death he began to hear confessions very early in the morning"; after Mass "again he went into the Confessional"; in the afternoon, and "during the rest of the day down to supper time," he heard confessions. After supper, "he heard the confessions of those Fathers who were to say the first Masses on the following morning," when he himself was no longer to be on earth. It was this extraordinary persevering service in so trying, so wearing a duty, for forty-five years, that enabled him to be the new Apostle of the Sacred City.[45]

When we pray, we allow the Spirit to unite us to Christ—in Christ—who carries us by his prayer into his Father's heart. St. Philip Neri began to live in and with the heart of God even here, while he walked on this earth. Like his prayers, our prayers are human prayers, and we do not pray alone. The Spirit intercedes for us to unite our prayers to the one prayer of Christ, who unites the things of earth to the things of heaven in himself (see Romans 8:26-39).

Christ works in and through our humanity by the Holy Spirit to draw us up with him to our heavenly homeland. He fills us with his Spirit to perform his works of love. He comes to us in our prayer to bring us to where he *is*: his Father's house.[46]

He Who Prays

Every Christian's prayer resounds from Christ's own prayer. Our prayers are not only gathered up in him but also begin in him. He is the beginning and the end, the first and the last, the Alpha and the Omega (Revelation 22:13). Our journey home to the Father begins in Jesus' prayer for his disciples.

When Jesus came to the seashore and first laid eyes on Simon Peter, James, and John, he was coming from "a lonely place" to which he had retreated (Luke 4:42). Jesus' call to his first disciples emerged from his solitude. "And . . . they left everything and followed him" (5:11).

When Jesus called his disciples and chose from among them the twelve apostles, he had spent the previous night alone in prayer. His call in the morning originated from his prayer in the night. Those who answered his call were the answer to Jesus' prayer (Luke 6:12-13).

When Jesus asked his disciples the decisive question of discipleship—"Who do you say that I am?"—it happened as "he was praying alone [and] the disciples were with him" (Luke 9:18, 20). His question came from his prayer, and his disciples' answer came in the context of his prayer. He was praying *alone*, and the disciples were *with him*. Theirs was a dialogue in prayer.

When faced with the fragility of Simon Peter's faith and the crisis that the first among the apostles would undergo through the temptations of Satan, Jesus told him, "I have prayed for you that your faith may not fail; and when you have turned again, strengthen your brethren" (Luke 22:32). Peter's infidelity and his conversion were wrapped in the prayer of Christ. The strength of Peter's faith, which would strengthen the others, was the fruit of Christ's prayer.

When Jesus begins to consummate his mission, in his prayer to his Father on the night before he died, he prays for his disciples. "I am praying for them; I am not praying for the world but for those whom you have given me, for they are yours; all mine are yours, and yours are mine, and I am glorified in them" (John 17:9-10). From the first day on the seashore, all who have answered his call have answered in response to Jesus' prayer. He prayed that they might respond freely in response to the Father moving their hearts—and respond these disciples did. As the culmination of his life's mission, Jesus offers to his Father the disciples for whom he prayed.

And when Jesus draws his prayer on earth to a close, his prayer passes through his disciples to those who believe in him through his disciples' preaching: "I do not pray for these only, but also for those who believe in me through their word" (John 17:20). The revolution of communion began in the words of Jesus' prayer to the Father in "a lonely place." These words will reverberate in all who come to believe in his name. Every disciple down through the centuries is the fruit of Jesus' prayer. Our prayers begin in him and redound to his prayers for us.

Christ's prayer is the source of our freedom. Freely he joined himself to us in all things, so that we might freely respond to his call. He prays for our response; he does not force it. His humility is his power, the power of divine freedom become human freedom. He who prays is free—free to hear and free to act. And disciples who pray are living testimonies to Christ, who prays for them.

Since our prayer begins in him, we must ask him to "teach us to pray" (Luke 11:1).

For Reflection

1. Peter faltered in entrusting himself to the Lord. Do you sometimes falter, wondering if Jesus really is who he says he is? How can Mary's example of quiet pondering help you trust more and more in the Lord?

2. Jesus has given all he has to us, promising to make a place for us in the Father's house. Do you find joy and hope in this promise? How does his promise encourage you to persevere in the challenges of daily life?

3. Before his death, Jesus prayed for those who would believe in him through the witness of his disciples. You are his disciple. Have you taken his prayer to heart? In what specific ways do you seek his abiding presence and direction so that you can bring him to others, filled with his joy?

Chapter Four

Learning How to Pray in Christ

Jesus teaches his disciples to pray. To learn from him, we must follow him and contemplate him, obeying his Father's command to "listen to him."

When people teach prayer in Jesus' name, their first duty is to present and embody the Lord whom they have come to trust and to love. In doing this, these teachers draw other disciples into intimacy with Jesus Christ.[47] Jesus is the supreme authority on prayer, because he enfolds those he claims into his own prayer. It matters that we ask *him*, trusting that he has "the words of eternal life" (John 6:68).

We ask him not only because he knows how to pray but also because he is his prayer. He offers himself to his Father as the only begotten Son. He raises up our humanity to the Father, because he has taken on our humanity as his own.

His prayer is who he is: the union of heaven and earth, of God and man. Those who desire to pray seek to be drawn into that union through him. To ask Christ to teach us to pray is to ask him to share himself with us, so that we might become one with him in his Father's love.

The first disciples of Jesus saw him pray time and time again—"as was his custom" (Luke 22:39). He preached and healed by day, and by night he prayed. The crowds were present for the preaching and miracles; in times of prayer, he was alone or, at least on occasion, only his disciples were present: "Now it happened that as he was praying alone the disciples were with him" (Luke 9:18). He is alone in prayer, *and* his disciples are with him. The crowds are not there.

It was on one such occasion that "one of his disciples said to him, 'Lord, teach us to pray'" (Luke 11:1). The disciple followed Jesus into prayer and contemplated him first, and then the disciple asked for Christ's teaching. He knew whom to ask. Moreover, contemplating Jesus moved this disciple to want to pray. So it is that "[b]y *contemplating* and hearing the Son, the master of prayer, the children learn to pray to the Father" (*Catechism* 2601).

In response to this specific request, Jesus teaches his disciples to pray, "*Our* Father" (Matthew 6:9, emphasis mine). Whose Father? Jesus teaches his disciples to call *his* Father *our* Father (see John 20:17). Disciples are thus taught to pray into the relationship with God the Father that Jesus alone may rightly call his own. He *is* the Son, and those who pray in him come to share in what he is. In Christ we become children of God.

Christian prayer is the exercise of coming to share in Christ's life. When contemplating him in the previous two chapters, we followed the Son of God in his descent to the fullness of our humanity and then in his ascent with our humanity to the glory of his Father's house. For disciples to pray into Christ means to take our share in both his descent and his ascent. As we will explore in this chapter, sharing in his descent means learning from him the right disposition for prayer. In the next chapter, we will learn how he empowers us to pray, to petition his Father in his name, and to speak boldly under the promise that he will hear us and unite our prayers with his own.

None of this is complicated, and all of it is challenging. That is because being joined to Christ in the right disposition for prayer means being humble, and humility is hard. It is hard in one way when we are young, in another way when we are old, and in all kinds of ways in between.

In the beloved children's book *The Giving Tree*, Shel Silverstein shows us a once trusting and joyful little boy who becomes a covetous and pompous adult, only to return in the end to the patient and long-suffering tree who has loved him throughout, giving of itself so thoroughly over the years that it is now nothing more than a stump. To rest again in the love of "the giving tree" requires the grown boy to settle down and be humble. It is not complicated, but it is challenging, and it is a long journey for the boy.

Our journey into the disposition of Christ, who gives us his prayer, is the ongoing journey of becoming a child of God who rests in his peace.

The Dispositions of Praying the Lord's Prayer

The Lord's Prayer contains all we need. This prayer is the Lord's, because the words Jesus gives to his disciples are words he received directly from his Father (see John 17:7). At the same time, the petitions that Jesus recites and hands over to his disciples come from the depths of his heart, where he knows the needs of his brothers and sisters whose humanity he shares (*Catechism* 2765). This single prayer is, at once, the revelation of the Father's will for us and of our own needs.

The Lord's Prayer is a summary of the entire gospel: the good news of Jesus Christ, who brings together in himself the things above with the things below. St. Augustine ventured to say, "Run through all the words of the holy prayers [in Scripture], and I do not think that you will find anything in them that is not contained and included in the Lord's Prayer."[48] St. Thomas Aquinas boasted not just of this prayer's completeness but also of its wisdom in setting out the proper order for a Christian's desires:

> The Lord's Prayer is the most perfect of prayers. . . . In it we ask, not only for all the things we can rightly desire, but also in the sequence that they should be desired. This prayer not only teaches us to ask for things, but also in what order we should desire them.[49]

Jesus hands over this proper ordering of things in seven petitions.[50] These petitions move from the desire for God, to the desire for daily needs and right relationship, to the desire for preservation from the power of evil. While reflecting on this singular prayer, Blessed Franz Jägerstätter marveled at its fullness but also at its simplicity and directness:

> When we look over the entire Our Father, we see that it actually contains only two major petitions and a minor one. That we enter into God's kingdom. That we remain out of the kingdom of sin. And between these two main parts there lies the small request, namely, that we receive daily bread.
>
> Therefore, when we devoutly pray the Our Father, we pray the paradigm prayer to which there is no equal. This prayer contains everything which human beings need in order to live happily in this world and also become eternally blessed![51]

Like St. Francis of Assisi and many other saints, Blessed Franz meditated on the petitions of the Lord's Prayer, seeking to deepen his understanding from the starting point of faith.[52] By not only praying these words but also seeking to learn what to desire through reflecting on their wisdom, disciples are ordered to God's own order in Christ. This is the truly human (and humane) order for faith, for hope, and for daily living in the way of love.

Jesus gives his disciples both the petitions to pray and the confidence to ask *his* Father for these things. Before praying these words in truth though, each disciple and the entire Church must offer something of themselves: humility. We must place ourselves in the right order relative to God. Simply put, we must enter into prayer confessing that we are *not* God, that we desire to be like him, and that we trust him (see *Catechism* 2784–85). *We* ask *him*.

In fact, praying each line of this prayer with a sincere heart inculcates the very humility it demands from us. The power of the Lord's Prayer is not just in who gives us this prayer or in what we are praying for but also in who we have to become to pray it in truth. This begins with the first words—"Our Father"—which beckon us to take our rightful, humble place as disciples who pray. This movement into the right disposition continues through each of the following petitions. We might recognize this more fully if we examine by faith how Jesus teaches us to pray.

Our Father

To call God "Father," you must become a child. This is the first, the most basic, and perhaps the only requirement for praying the Lord's Prayer. We do not approach God as an equal, nor as someone who possesses titles or honors that God must respect. The opening words of the Lord's Prayer incline us to become small. The way to approach God is as one who is dependent, who cannot provide for yourself, but who also knows that you are loved with paternal affection.

When Jesus prays, he never fails to call God "Father." Jesus knows who God is, and he also knows who he himself is: he is the Son of the Father. In teaching his disciples to pray, Jesus opens for us both this knowledge of God and this gift of who he is. He instructs his disciples to call God "Father" and, by doing so, requires us to become the children God desires us to become.

If you look for the word "Father" in the Gospels, you will soon notice how often this word appears. Jesus never ceases teaching his disciples and even the crowds to approach and call upon God as Father. In fact, when his disciples were becoming covetous and pompous, seeking after their own titles and honors, Jesus chastened them for acting and scheming like those who are wise in the ways of the world. Disciples cannot approach God in such a way; in fact, they will never ascend to God if they do not humble themselves first: "Truly, I say to you, unless you turn and become like children, you will never enter the kingdom of heaven. Whoever humbles himself like this child, he is the greatest in the kingdom of heaven" (Matthew 18:3-4).

Only children may pray to God. To enter into Jesus' prayer, disciples must become children.[53]

Who Art in Heaven

"Seek first his kingdom" (Matthew 6:33). What Jesus eventually teaches his disciples in regard to the anxieties of life, he first teaches them in prayer. The one whom we call Father is neither reduced to nor limited by the many things we find around us in this world. He is not of this world. He is above us but bends down to us in our lowliness.

Jesus himself is that bending down. In being so, he inclines us to lift up our eyes and our hearts to his Father, reigning in heaven. Christians, who have died with Christ in Baptism, must do one thing if we are to follow him into glory: set our hearts. We seek first God's kingdom. We desire that kingdom most of all, because in desiring it, we desire God himself. He reigns in heaven; our dwelling with him *is* heaven.[54]

Seeking God in heaven is a confession of our present lowliness and homelessness. We are below; he is above. Where we are now is not where we are called to be in the fullness of time. We are seekers: we seek God. That puts us in the position of longing to dwell with him, where he is, even as he has come to dwell with us, where we are: "And the Word became flesh and dwelt among us" (John 1:14).

In teaching us to call upon God as Father "in heaven," Jesus orients his disciples to the end of all our desiring and to our final, true homeland. As St. Paul teaches on Christ's behalf, "seek the things that are above, where Christ is, seated at the right hand of God. Set your minds on things that are above, not on things that are on earth" (Colossians 3:1-2).

Hallowed Be Thy Name

The name of God is a gift. It is not merely a placeholder for his presence, like a sign that points to a thing that is not otherwise there. No, the name of God is the presence and the action of God.

When Moses asked God for his name, God said, "I AM WHO I AM" (Exodus 3:14). To invoke his name is to encounter his presence. But the other translation of the Hebrew name that God gives Moses is something like "I Will Be What I Will Be." To invoke the holy name in that sense means to accept the works of the Lord as revealing who God is, because what God does *for us* shows us who God is. This all comes to us as a gift: God's presence, God's action.

Receiving the gift of the name of God entails receiving and entering into Jesus Christ. Indeed, as Joseph Ratzinger (later Pope Benedict XVI) wonderfully expressed:

> The name of Jesus brings the mysterious name at the burning bush to its fulfillment; now we can see that God had not said all that he had to say but had interrupted his discourse for a time. This is because the name "Jesus" in its Hebrew form includes the word "Yahweh" and adds a further element to it: God "saves."
>
> "I am who I am"—thanks to Jesus, this now means: "I am the one who saves you." His Being is salvation.[55]

Jesus instructs us to revere the name of God—to observe and remember this name's holiness—because this is the presence and this is the action that saves us. We forget who and what we are if we take this name for granted, if we fail to recognize the God who comes to us, if we do not remember that we are the ones whom he saves. Jesus' name is the name "which is above every other name" (Philippians 2:9), because he is the Father's love given to us, and he draws us in himself to the heart of the Father. In Jesus we call God "*our* Father," but that is never something we earn or can claim as our own. It is a gift, which we are given in the name of Christ.

Praying to God *by name* is therefore always preceded by the gift of God to us. We are recipients before we are petitioners; we are found before we seek. To pray in Christ is an exercise in gratitude: he has given us the power to pray through his own presence and action.

Thy Kingdom Come

To anticipate participating in the reign of God means laying aside our own schemes for building our little kingdoms and organizing our worlds the way we would like them to be. To herald the coming of God's kingdom means confessing the provisional nature of our plans and welcoming the death of our private authority, our myth of "self-rule." In Christ, disciples share in God's reign, not vice versa.

The cofounder of the Catholic Worker movement, Dorothy Day, was especially keen on this point. She once wrote that "you can strip yourself, you can be stripped, but still you will reach out like an octopus to seek your own comfort, your untroubled time, your ease, your refreshment."[56] All these are ways of clinging to your own "self-rule." Day urges us to stop being octopuses reaching for control and instead learn to receive God's rule, God's wisdom, God's way.

She glimpsed something of this wondrous death to self in the tireless care of poor mothers, who practice prizing their children's well-being over their own private preferences, even to the point of utter exhaustion:

Sometimes the only thing that keeps a woman going is the necessity of taking care of her young. . . . [T]he young ones are dragging at her skirts, clamoring for something—food, clothing, shelter, occupation. She is carried outside herself. . . . [S]he has a rule of life which involves others.[57]

Parents who place the needs of their children first have already practiced letting go of their own lust for control.

To welcome the reign of a king means to welcome his authority, his customs, his ways and decrees. The disciple's "rule of life" is God's rule. It involves placing yourself in the position of fitting in and adapting, changing yourself as necessary. It also means being ready to be judged for the ways in which your own ways are not God's ways, and your thoughts not his thoughts (see Isaiah 55:8-9).

When the younger son returned to his Father's household, in Jesus' parable of the prodigal, the elder son refused to come inside (see Luke 15:25-32). He did not like the terms of the household. He had other ideas and other plans. He did not welcome the ways of his father but instead demanded that his father adapt to his ways.

For that elder son to truly pray for the coming of his father's reign, he would have to let go of his own desire to reign supreme. He would have to stop reaching out like an octopus for his own comfort and his own arrangements and his own preferred way of doing things. He must die to himself to enter his father's household on his father's terms.

Jesus really does know the human heart.

Thy Will Be Done

The only way to prepare for God's unending reign is to do his will now. Again, the Christian at prayer encounters sacrifice: not my will first, not any other's will first, but God's will first. In the end, there are only two ways: either we say to God, "Thy will be done!" or God says to us, "*Thy* will be done!"[58] If we choose to separate ourselves from God, he will not force himself on us. But if we choose to live in Christ with God, then we must choose his will.

What Jesus commands, he first does. To his disciples he says, "My food is to do the will of him who sent me" (John 4:34). To the devil, who tempts him to satisfy his own hunger, he says,

> Man shall not live by bread alone,
> but by every word that proceeds from the mouth of God. (Matthew 4:4; see Luke 4:4; Deuteronomy 8:3).

Then, in the Garden of Gethsemane, when tempted to preserve his own life, Jesus says, "Father, . . . not my will, but yours, be done" (Luke 22:42). Each day and through all our days, the will of God is the true sustenance of disciples, for the Father's will sustains and motivates Christ himself.

The humility to ask for and wait for the Father's will to be given: this is the painful predicament in which the Lord's Prayer places disciples. Before seeking bread or any other created thing, we are to wait upon God's word. All other plans yield at this petition. The one who prays thus puts himself in the position of having to hear and obey.

Give Us This Day Our Daily Bread

Asking for bread changes what bread is. It is no longer just bread, but it becomes bread given. The bread itself is a gift.

When the Israelites grumbled against God in the desert because they did not have enough to eat, God gave them bread: "I will rain bread from heaven for you" (Exodus 16:4). It was bread from the sky, it was bread to sustain them on their journey, and it was their daily bread. They called it *manna*, which literally means "What is it?" (16:15). They would learn through practice that this bread was not just bread: it was an education in trust, an invitation to cling to the Lord, and a lesson in what it means to welcome him.

There were three conditions for receiving this bread: first, the Israelites had to gather the bread daily; second, they could only gather what they needed, not an excess to store; and third, they could not gather on the Sabbath but instead had to gather a double portion the day before. Was God being stingy or difficult? No. The point was not just that they receive the bread they needed but rather that they recognize that it was bread *given to them*. They were receiving from the hand of God.

If you do not ask daily, you forget that your life is in fact sustained daily and that very little of that is by your own doing. If you store up an excess, you can become self-satisfied and begin to rely on yourself: you stop asking for what you need. And if you are really going to trust in the one who gives you what you need, you will listen to his word and gather double when he says "double" and not at all when he says "not at all." The Israelites ate *manna* in the desert, but they did not live on bread alone. They lived on bread given—given according to God's will.

To ask God for bread is to do more than seek bread as your daily sustenance. It is to ask God to be a Father to you, and it is to trust that he will respond to you as his beloved child.

> [W]hat man of you, if his son asks him for bread, will give him a stone? . . . If you then, who are evil, know how to give good gifts to your children, how much more will your Father who is in heaven give good things to those who ask him! (Matthew 7:9, 11).

The bread is not the point; God's paternal and providential care for you is the point. Disciples become like Jesus when we trust his Father to be *our* Father. And by asking, we receive (see Matthew 7:8).

Forgive Us Our Trespasses

Petitioning God to forgive our sins entails a double confession for disciples: it is a confession of our own sinfulness and a confession of God's merciful love.

To beg for forgiveness is to tell the truth. As St. Augustine proclaimed in the first line of his *Confessions*, "Great are you, O Lord, and exceedingly worthy of praise."[59] We accept our own need and lowliness in proclaiming God's greatness, and we give praise to God by asking for his mercy. Our request for the mercy of forgiveness puts us in the position of accepting God for who God has revealed himself to be: "a God merciful and gracious, slow to anger, and abounding in mercy and faithfulness, keeping merciful love for thousands, forgiving iniquity and transgression and sin" (Exodus 34:6-7).

There is no blank to fill in with this plea. We do not merely ask to be forgiven for the sins we recognize and name. Christ teaches his disciples to seek forgiveness for all trespasses: for what we have done and what we have failed to do; for the sins we know and the sins we ignore; for the sins against God and the ways in which we harm our neighbors, which God absorbs as being done against him in Christ (see Matthew 25:41-45). Disciples must err on the side of asking forgiveness, even when we are unaware of our sins.

This plea for forgiveness is an act of trust that God, who in his Word created all things, will also mend and restore all things; that God, who said "let there be light," will probe the depths of our hearts and reveal what is hidden; that the Son of God, who said, "Father, forgive them; for they know not what they do," was speaking about us (Luke 23:34). Christ prays for our forgiveness, and we join in his prayer when we ask to receive it.

As We Forgive Those Who Trespass against Us

Jesus teaches his disciples to ask his Father for a share in his pain and his joy. This petition forces disciples to abandon our own ways and accept God's ways, seeking to become what we otherwise would not choose to be and to do what we otherwise would not choose to do. We consent to absorbing others' offenses and exchanging their curses for our blessings.

Love your enemies, and do good, and lend, expecting nothing in return; and your reward will be great, and you will be sons of the Most High; for he is kind to the ungrateful and the selfish. Be merciful, even as your Father is merciful. (Luke 6:35-36; see also Matthew 5:44-48)

Becoming merciful is the condition for receiving the Father's mercy. Jesus teaches his disciples that we cannot ask for forgiveness if we are unwilling to learn how to forgive (see Matthew 18:23-35). Forgiving is the condition for being forgiven, because what God gives in his mercy is the gift of becoming like him, turning our hearts of stone into hearts of flesh so we might love one another (see Jeremiah 31:33; Ezekiel 11:19; 36:26; John 13:34; 15:12; Hebrews 8:10).

It is in acts of forgiveness that ordinary people like us are revealed to be most like God. Each act of forgiveness is its own mystery. That mystery is the mystery of becoming merciful like the Father (see Luke 6:36), which is Christ's desire for each of us.

And so let us look at the testimony of Epiphanie Mukamusoni—a victim of the 1994 Rwandan genocide. We can do nothing but marvel at the divine power that courses through her as she forgives François Ntambra, the man who trespassed against her:

He killed my child, then he came to ask me pardon. I immediately granted it to him because he did not do it by himself—he was haunted by the devil. I was pleased by the way he testified to the crime instead of keeping it in hiding, because it hurts if someone keeps hiding a crime he committed against you. Before, when I had not yet granted him pardon, he could not come close to me. I treated him like my enemy. But now, I would rather treat him like my own child.[60]

Mercy is the coin of the kingdom of God, and Epiphanie is one of the King's cherished emissaries.

Lead Us Not into Temptation

The only temptation is to trust in ways that are not God's ways, including our own private ways:

> Trust in the LORD with all your heart,
>   and do not rely on your own insight. (Proverbs 3:5)

Asking God to lead us is both a petition and the fulfillment of that petition: we ask God to take the lead, and in the same breath we follow his lead.

Rather than self-doubt, this is a plea of self-knowledge. Jesus teaches his disciples to accept the knowledge that, on our own, we falter. Seeking to direct myself is the root of all sin: the first and final temptation. It is to live as if I were my own god.

To call upon God means to entrust ourselves to him. Those who seek God as Father never leave the valley of humility, where lives a healthy distrust of our own wisdom. St. Paul, who prayed in Christ time and time again, learned to see ever more clearly that "I do not do what I want, but I do the very thing I hate" (Romans 7:15). He distrusted his own understanding and trusted in God, whose power and wisdom are revealed in Christ alone (see 1 Corinthians 1:24).

Deliver Us from Evil

Evil is the absence of God. In that absence, Satan comes to dwell, he who always desires our alienation from God. Those who pray in Christ ask God to be present to them.

The conclusion of the Lord's Prayer recapitulates what each line of the prayer inclines disciples to seek: the communion of the Son with his Father, whom Christ gives us as *our* Father. We ask God to drive out the evil within and around us with his own presence. To ask to be delivered is to beg for what we cannot do for ourselves.

We ask the Father to make us his children, who share in his life. We ask him to reveal his name to us: his presence and his action. We ask him to draw us into his heavenly household, transferring us from the dominion of darkness into the kingdom of his beloved Son, where God is all in all (see 1 Corinthians 15:28; Colossians 1:13; Revelation 21:22-26).

Christ, the Way to the Father

The Lord's Prayer is the perfect prayer: by praying this prayer what we request is already fulfilled. To pray the words that Jesus gave us, we must become the kind of people we pray to be. We ask to become God's children in Christ, who wait for his kingdom and give allegiance to his will, who seek his nourishment always, who follow his ways, who ward off temptation, and who are not removed from God.

We ask, and it is given. This prayer is not magic, and it does not force God's hand. Rather God has given all things in Christ, and by this prayer, we practice receiving what he has given us.

Commenting on the routine of prayer that may otherwise be taken for granted, St. John Henry Newman seeks to rekindle awe in disciples who are given the words of Jesus to pray. We find in these words "the force of association in undoing the evil of past years, and recalling us to the innocence of children." The saint appeals to a renewed sense of wonder in Christians:

> [S]urely there are few of us, if we dwelt on the thought, but would feel it a privilege to use, as we do (for instance, in the Lord's Prayer), the very petitions which Christ spoke. He gave the prayer and used it. His Apostles used it; all the Saints ever since have used it. When we use it, we join company with them. . . . Thus does the Lord's Prayer bring us near to Christ, and to His disciples in every age.[61]

Christ gives us his prayer, so that all who pray these words may say, "Our Father," together in him, with one another. Praying in Christ makes us one, as he gives his Father to us. His prayer makes us the Father's children.

The way to the Father is open wide in Christ: "I am the way, and the truth, and the life; no one comes to the Father, but by me" (John 14:6), and again, "I am the door; if any one enters by me, he will be saved, and will go in and out and find pasture" (10:9). Christ is the one who emptied himself of everything in order to share in our humanity. His humility is our opening.

To enter into his prayer, we follow his way of humility: letting go of riches and titles and status; becoming beggars or rather children in need. Our Father wants us to rest in him; we must simply let ourselves do so, with all that we have and all that we are. Only those who bend down to become like little children enter into the Lord's Prayer, as if passing through the eye of a needle (see Matthew 19:23-26; Mark 10:23-27; Luke 18:24-27).

The Parables of Prayer

Jesus' parables are part of the revelation of who he is, which is to say that the parables serve to show who God is. They also show who we are and the struggle and drama of our communion with God. Jesus is that union in person, and he draws his hearers from where we are toward the union with God that he offers. Receiving his parables through the medium of Scripture, we hear him drawing us to his Father. We become the direct recipients of his words, if only we are willing to listen.

We ought to study each of Jesus' parables, as each one and all of them together never cease to stretch, correct, and nourish us. But if we were to select only a few of the parables to study in depth as we continue to ask Christ to teach us how to pray, we would do well to fix our attention on three parables on prayer in the Gospel of Luke, which all follow the Lord's Prayer.[62]

These three parables serve as Jesus' sermons on the prayer he has just handed over to his disciple; through these images, he continues to form his disciples in the Lord's Prayer. For his disciples today, it is by dwelling with Christ's words in these parables that we come to the humility and the posture of open-ness that we must embody in order to pray in him.

The Friend at Midnight

> And he said to them, "Which of you who has a friend will go to him at midnight and say to him, 'Friend, lend me three loaves; for a friend of mine has arrived on a journey, and I have nothing to set before him'; and he will answer from within, 'Do not bother me; the door is now shut, and my children are with me in bed; I cannot get up and give you anything'? I tell you, though he will not get up and give him anything because he is his friend, yet because of his importunity he will rise and give him whatever he needs." (Luke 11:5-8)

This parable immediately follows Jesus' gift of the Lord's Prayer to his disciples, and it is expressly connected to that prayer by the request for bread (11:3, 5). On first pass, it seems that it is the persistence of the petitioner that turns the friend's negative response into a positive response, as if the man cozy in his bed is stung into charity through the obnoxiousness of the man at the door. Shall we annoy God with our prayers, like inconsiderate neighbors or whiny children?

Maybe there is something to that, but it puts a lot of weight on the word translated as "importunity," meaning something like persistence (11:8). Indeed, as Jesus says, it is the petitioner's "importunity" that makes the difference. The Greek word here is *anaideia*, which appears nowhere else in the New Testament and only once in the Greek translation of the Old Testament (see Sirach 25:22). In other literature from this period, all its uses are negative, conveying not the positive quality of persistence but rather the negative quality of "shamelessness," as in one who is rude and does not abide by the proper rules of conduct. The man at the door is rude—shamelessly rude.[63]

As we think about the parable more deeply, we might recognize that nothing within it speaks to the man's repeated knocking or repeated petitioning. There is nothing in these verses or in the ones that immediately follow that speak to persistence. He asks once, and afterward the explanation of the parable focuses on the importance of asking, not on the repetitious nature of requests.

On its own terms—in Jesus' words, as Luke presents them—the shamelessness of the man seems key. This friend in bed gets up even though nothing about the man's request is proper, timely, or in good form. The man at the door must have some remarkable trust in his friend's generosity if he comes expecting him to answer a plea like this. His shamelessness is like an inverse reflection of his confidence in his friend's readiness to respond.

What is Jesus revealing in this parable? He is not primarily revealing something about the man who offers the petition or the manner in which this man petitions his sleeping friend. Instead Jesus is drawing our attention to the sleeping friend himself. If he—who is cozy in bed, who has put out the lights and locked up for the night, who is surrounded by his children, whose day is most certainly done—if *he* will get up to respond to his needy friend's plea, even when his friend asks in a totally shameful way and goes about it all wrong, then "*how much more* will the heavenly Father give the Holy Spirit to those who ask him!" (Luke 11:13, emphasis added).

Jesus is moving us, his listeners, from weaker to stronger through this "how much more." The response of the sleeping friend is the weak part of the analogy; the response of the heavenly Father is the strong part. The parable teaches the certainty of a God who hears our prayers.[64] The important thing for those who are needy is to ask. Trust him as a friend but even more as a father (see Luke 11:11-13).

"Our Father, who art in heaven, . . . give us this day our daily bread."

The Unjust Judge

> And he told them a parable, to the effect that they ought always to pray and not lose heart. He said, "In a certain city there was a judge who neither feared God nor regarded man; and there was a widow in that city who kept coming to him and saying, 'Vindicate me against my adversary.' For a while he refused; but afterward he said to himself, 'Though I neither fear God nor regard man, yet because this widow bothers me, I will vindicate her, or she will wear me out by her continual coming.'" (Luke 18:1-5)

It is not just anyone who comes to the judge seeking justice but specifically a widow. In the ancient world, widows were generally powerless and vulnerable. Along with orphans and foreigners, widows required the support and protection of others.[65] She who comes begging does not have rights or honors or titles to flaunt. All she has is her plea, and she offers this plea again and again. She cries out for justice.

The judge is truly wicked. By his own admission, he cares for neither God nor man. He follows his own rule and utterly neglects the twin commandment to love God and love your neighbor. He is not only without compassion and devoid of mercy; he also neglects the basic conditions of justice, even though he has a particular responsibility to uphold them. He is slothful in the face of what is true and good. His heart is as stone, and his will is as molasses.

Nevertheless, the widow persists. What else can she do? She knows that she is without power; her well-being is in his hands. What she yearns for has not come, but she desires it without ceasing, and in her desperation she continues to ask. Her desire finally moves the unjust judge—not that he is moved to compassion but only moved to action. The fidelity of her desire—seeking nothing less—is powerful.

To whom does Jesus tell this parable? To those who have asked when the kingdom of God is coming—a question first posed by the Pharisees (Luke 17:20) but then taken up as if asked by his disciples. To these disciples he says, "The days are coming when you will desire to see one of the days of the Son of man, and you will not see it" (17:22). They will soon desire what has not come. Will they persist in desiring? Will they continue to ask?

The widow begs that justice may reign on earth for her. The disciples are to beg that the Lord's kingdom may come, ful-filling God's will on earth. They are to be the ones who "[cry] out with a loud voice, 'O Sovereign Lord, holy and true, how long?" (Revelation 6:10).

If the unjust judge, who is without compassion and devoid of mercy, acts on the widow's desire, *how much more* will "God vindicate his elect, who cry to him day and night?" (Luke 18:7). The degree of difference between the unjust judge and God is even greater here than the difference between the sleepy friend and God. God not only heeds the petitions of those who ask but also remains faithful to his promises, fulfilling the desires of those who long for him. The only real question is "When the Son of man comes, will he find faith on earth?" (18:8).

God's deliverance is certain, but will those who need it persist in desiring the presence and action of God? Will we make that desire our own and cling to it when fulfillment is delayed?

Persistence is proven and built through continually asking. For those without power, who know themselves to be meek, asking is the only power they have.

"Thy kingdom come, thy will be done, on earth as it is in heaven. . . . [D]eliver us from evil."

The Pharisee and the Tax Collector

He also told this parable to some who trusted in themselves that they were righteous and despised others. "Two men went up into the temple to pray, one a Pharisee and the other a tax collector. The Pharisee stood and prayed thus with himself, 'God, I thank you that I am not like other men, extortioners, unjust, adulterers, or even like this tax collector. I fast twice a week, I give tithes of all that I get.' But the tax collector, standing far off, would not even lift up his eyes to heaven, but beat his breast, saying, 'God, be merciful to me a sinner!'" (Luke 18:9-13)

The Pharisee and the tax collector are alike in that they both go up to the Temple to pray. They go to the same place to do the same thing. Yet both the content and the manner of their prayer separate them. The Pharisee's prayer is long, while the description of his posture is brief: he is upright. The tax collector's prayer is brief, while the description of his posture is long: he stands far off, his eyes are downcast, he beats his breast.[66]

The Pharisee prays "with himself": he is the content of his own prayer. He prays in thanksgiving for being just the way he is: he finds satisfaction in himself and looks down on those who do not measure up to his presumed righteousness. He is the elder brother who despises the prodigality of his lesser brother and stands upright against the lowliness of such a sinner.[67]

The tax collector, by contrast, prays for God's mercy. Thus he makes a double confession: he confesses God's greatness as the one who is merciful, and he confesses that he himself is a sinner who needs this mercy. He does not name his sins; rather he claims himself a sinner and names God as the one who is merciful (see Exodus 34:6-7). He is a man who needs help with everything.

By their postures and their prayers, these two men not only reveal themselves but also present their different images of God. The Pharisee makes God into the approver of the dutiful, the contented, and the scrupulous. The tax collector addresses God as the one who hears the cry of the poor and responds in mercy. Only one of these is the true God. Who has God shown himself to be? What is his name?

The man who bent low in humility, under the weight of his guilt, was "justified" and even "exalted" (Luke 18:14). He passed into the way of Christ. Conversely, the Pharisee sought to exalt himself; he chose his own way, rather than Christ's. The Pharisee was large in his own estimation, while the tax collector pleaded like a little child.

Not only does the Pharisee fail to recognize his sinfulness and ask for forgiveness, but he also neglects to have mercy on the sinner in his midst. He ridicules rather than cares for the tax collector. He certainly does not pray for him: he has too much of himself in his prayer for that. He has no room for God's mercy and thus cannot become merciful. He denies the gift.

The Pharisee relies on his own wisdom; the tax collector yields to the power and wisdom of God as his only hope. The tax collector cannot direct himself, let alone save himself—and he knows it. So he puts himself into the hands of God.

". . . Hallowed be thy name. . . . And forgive us our trespasses, as we forgive those who trespass against us, and lead us not into temptation."

Ask in Prayer

What Jesus says in conclusion about the Pharisee and the tax collector unveils the bedrock truth about the disposition necessary to pray into Christ: "Every one who exalts himself will be humbled, but he who humbles himself will be exalted"

(Luke 18:14). Jesus is the humility of the only begotten Son; he is the one who "did not count equality with God a thing to be grasped, but emptied himself" (Philippians 2:6-7). He descended, and the Father raised him up. For those who seek to join Christ in his union with the Father, the key is to become like a little child. Then the Father can raise us up into his arms—as a father does.

When we ask Jesus to teach us how to pray, he teaches what he himself is and what he himself does. He never fails to call God "Father," he never stops accepting himself as the Father's Son, and he never ceases to desire what his Father seeks to give him. As he teaches his disciples how to pray, he teaches us how to enter into his prayer. His prayer is always offered in humility and truth, and so must ours be.

Jesus not only does what he commands but also fulfills what he promises. "Therefore I tell you, whatever you ask in prayer, believe that you receive it, and you will" (Mark 11:24). And again, "Whatever you ask in my name, I will do it, that the Father may be glorified in the Son; if you ask anything in my name, I will do it" (John 14:13-14; see John 15:7; 16:23; Matthew 21:22).

Christ's confidence in the Father is offered to his disciples. That is his gift to us, but the essential responsibility remains: he commands *us* to "ask in prayer" and "ask in my name."

To ask in prayer means to ask as a child, as a beggar, as one who confesses God's greatness and our own lowliness. It means learning to desire the right things in the right order and to keep desiring even when fulfillment is delayed. To ask in the name of Christ means to ask in the name of him who calls God "Father" and to receive his Father as *our* Father. It does not include babbling as the pagans do, or flaunting our worthiness, or trying to cajole God into our ways (see Matthew 6:5-15). Rather we must trust him as the merciful Father whom Jesus reveals him to be. Christ teaches us both the content and the manner of prayer in his name.

The disposition of humility is nearly everything, as we let God be God. But our work is not just in humbling; it is also in boldness. We rise up. We ask. We are responsible in prayer. And Christ hears us.

For Reflection

1. If the Lord's Prayer contains all we need, then it can be a source of peace in times of trouble. Do you turn to this prayer in your daily life? How could meditating on the petitions in this prayer encourage you and give you hope? And can this prayer form you to give hope to others?

2. In simplicity, ask the Lord to grant you the gift of humility. In what ways can humility—understanding who you are in relation to who God is—create a sturdy foundation for prayer in your life?

3. How have you experienced the gift of forgiveness in your life? When has someone else's forgiveness changed you, and when have you forgiven someone else? How would fully embracing God's forgiveness change the way you bring the gospel to others? How would receiving forgiveness free you to be a child of God?

CHAPTER FIVE

Lifting Up Our Prayers in Christ

Jesus prayed. Jesus taught his disciples to pray. Jesus wants his disciples to follow him into prayer. He wants us to share in his offering, as he gives all we have to his Father and gives everything from his Father to us. This exchange—this act of union—is his prayer. "I came that [you] might have life, and have it abundantly" (John 10:10). The point then is to live. We are to live in prayer.

Prayer is obedience to Christ, and it is the freedom of Christ. This is the way to salvation. He desires those he claims as his own to receive and heed the will of his Father in heaven, and thereby to discover the true freedom of the children of God (see John 8:34-38; Romans 8:14-23).

John, the beloved disciple, was the only apostle to live to old age. When all the others had been martyred, he alone remained.

In the time given to him, he pondered the mysteries of the love of Christ. He practiced doing what Christ commanded him to do: "Abide in my love" (John 15:9; see 1 John 2:23-25, 28).

To be claimed by Jesus is to be ransomed from the slavery of sin. To pray as he taught us to pray is to accept the freedom he offers: the freedom of his Father's love. As St. John testifies to the beloved community,

> See what love the Father has given us, that we should be called children of God; and so we are. . . . Beloved, we are God's children now; it does not yet appear what we shall be, but we know that when he appears we shall be like him, for we shall see him as he is. (1 John 3:1-2)

We pray our way to becoming like Christ, for he has given us his prayer as our own.

Jesus directs his disciples to "ask in prayer" and to "ask in my name." He draws us into his prayer. He is the one who prayed, "Father, forgive them," and, "Father, . . . let this chalice pass from me," and, "Holy Father, keep them in your name," and, "Father, I thank you that you have heard me" (Luke 23:34; Matthew 26:39; John 17:11; 11:41). He is the Son who never ceases reaching out to his Father. He gives his disciples a share in his sonship, he forms his disciples in prayer, and then he frees his disciples to address themselves to his Father as *our* Father.

"Ask in prayer," he tells us; "ask in my name," he implores. He beseeches us to join him in the love of his Father: to listen and speak, to weep and exclaim, to plead and praise as children of God.

The point of learning about prayer is not to keep learning about prayer; the point is to actually pray. During a retreat at the Abbey of Gethsemane in Kentucky, a group of us were talking to a Trappist monk, Fr. Matthew Kelty. He had been a worldly man, a man of letters, and a man steeped in New England culture prior to entering the monastery. So I asked him, "What was it like for *you* to enter the monastery?"

Fr. Matthew responded, "Well, the first thing is you just have to learn how to do everything. You have to learn how and when to eat, how and when to sleep, how and when to pray, how and when to work. There are all these steps in monastic life that you just don't know, and it takes a whole year before you feel like you are starting to get it all." He stopped speaking, and a bit of silence followed. Eventually I said, "So then what? What happens after a year?" His eyes sparkled with mirth as he responded, "Well, baby, then it's time to dance."

Christ teaches his disciples—*us!*—to pray so that we might actually pray. He keeps teaching us throughout our lives, and we keep learning. But at some point, it is also time to dance. Prayer is Christ's gift to us; actually praying is our response and our responsibility.

In contemplating the descent of the Son of God, we are formed to his humility: we learn the dispositions of children who pray. When we contemplate the ascent of the risen Christ, who clings to our humanity, we are thereby formed to offer up everything of our own humanity to "our Father, who art in heaven." Christ has *already* offered all of humanity to his Father; when we join in his prayer, we allow ourselves to be caught up in his offering.

This is part of the freedom of the children of God. Christ does not take us by force. He gives us the freedom to go with him. As St. John Henry Newman put it, "See, He offers you His hand; He is rising; rise with Him."[68]

Another part of the freedom of the children of God is that we can and ought to address everything about ourselves to the Father through Christ. Nothing is off limits. Christ's love determines the boundaries of prayer, and he has loved unto the end (see John 13:1). We are free to pray with all of it, in his name.

"The praying heart," Jean Corbon writes, "discovers that its true space is the ongoing event of the Ascension. . . . [T]his fiber of our humanity is no longer simply our own but belongs also to him who has assumed it, and who died and rose for us."[69]

"Christ's ascension marks the definitive entrance of Jesus' humanity into God's heavenly domain" (*Catechism* 665). Jesus is indeed seated at the right hand of his Father, and his humanity is there in glory. He beckons us, with all that we are, to ascend in him, with him, and through him. We are to lift up our hearts without anxiety and "by prayer and supplication with thanksgiving let [our] requests be made known to God" (Philippians 4:6).

In this final chapter of our study and growth into Christ at prayer, we will discern how the Father receives our prayers in his beloved Son. At the same time, we will witness the boldness that is called forth from us as disciples in prayer, even and especially in the midst of our own and other people's sufferings. From the first to the last sign of Jesus' glory, through the words and conditions that he allows us to offer up in him, all the way to the raising of our bodies and souls as one complete prayer—let us marvel together at the grace of our Lord and Savior, who gives us the gift of prayer.

Listening to Our Blessed Mother

> On the third day there was a marriage at Cana in Galilee, and the mother of Jesus was there. Jesus also was invited to the marriage, with his disciples. When the wine failed, the mother of Jesus said to him, "They have no wine." And Jesus said to her, "O woman, what have you to do with me? My hour has not yet come." His mother said to the servants, "Do whatever he tells you." (John 2:1-5)[70]

Mary's was the first voice that Jesus heard, hidden as he was in her womb. At the wedding of an unnamed bride and groom, Jesus heard her voice again. She troubled him, she asked him, she nearly commanded him; and he listened to her and acted on her word.

The primary tension in Jesus' life and earthly ministry is awaiting the appointed "hour" when the fullness of glory will be revealed in him. This is the glory of his Father, who receives from his Son the gift of the humanity he has taken on. In this glory, eternal life comes to all those Jesus claims as his own.

In his prayer to the Father at the conclusion of the Last Supper and immediately preceding his arrest, Jesus confesses that "the hour has come" (John 17:1). The full revelation of the union of humanity with God is gathered up in the prayer he offers then.

In the years preceding his full and final prayer at the appointed time, the Gospel of John tells us, Jesus performed seven signs that point to the glory that is to come in him and through him.[71] These signs anticipated what would later be revealed in full. The first of the seven signs was performed at the wedding at Cana in Galilee, and it came at Mary's behest.

Jesus tells his Mother in response to her plea, "My hour has not yet come." The time is not right, as with a friend who comes knocking and begging in the middle of the night. Nevertheless Mary inclines him to act before his appointed hour. Other guests and servants besides Mary know that the wine has run out, but no one else yet knows to trust completely in Jesus' compassion and power. To everyone else, the end of the wine is a problem without a remedy. To Mary, it is an occasion to petition her Son.

Mary is attentive enough to recognize the need at hand and bold enough to do something about it. But in her boldness, she is also aware of her limitation. Like a widow pleading before a judge, she knows that true power is in the hands of the one she approaches. She offers him her petition, and then she yields to his wisdom, directing everyone else, "Do whatever he tells you."

Her petition is brief: she merely brings the need to the one whom she trusts. She does not indulge in empty shows of piety or flaunt her righteousness, as would a Pharisee who is oh so pleased with himself. Instead she claims the need, she offers it to Jesus, and then she waits for him to act.

What then does she see? Yes, she sees him change water into wine with nothing but his voice. But she also sees him who is the Word made flesh allow her concern to affect him. She sees that he hears her prayer.

The servants who fill the six jars with water discover that something has changed. The head steward who tastes the wine discovers its fine quality. The groom discovers that he is inexplicably fortunate. But none of them witness the full sign.

Mary is the true witness. While all the others marvel at the wine, she is the first to see that God in his power and wisdom is attentive to the needs she offers. The water made wine is the sign of her prayer offered to the Father through the Son.

The sign Jesus works points to and makes present the fullness of glory yet to come. This revelation of glory is about both his Father in heaven and his mother on earth, who is a creature like us and the one from whom the Word of God received a share in our humanity. In Jesus, God hears and acts on the needs of his people, just as in Jesus, the faith and works of God's people help usher in the glory of God.

Mary is not just a passive recipient of God's action; rather she perceives the need, and she offers the petition to her Son. Her prayer is enfolded in what Jesus brings about. This wedding at Cana in Galilee is a sign of the union of God and humanity in Christ.

The glory to be revealed in Christ is that God not only saves his people but also makes his people agents of salvation. Praying into Christ, we disciples are made to be like God. We perceive needs, and we act on them by offering our petitions in trust.

Making Our Petitions Known

Mary trusted, Jesus responded, and "his disciples believed in him" (John 2:11). They believed because they had seen, as they discovered what it means to "have life in his name" (20:31). Those disciples who went to the wedding at Cana in Galilee with Jesus glimpsed what he would continue to show and teach them:

> Truly, truly, I say to you, he who believes in me will also do the works that I do; and greater works than these will he do, because I go to the Father. Whatever you ask in my name, I will do it, that the Father may be glorified in the Son; if you ask anything in my name, I will do it. . . .
> . . . [A]sk, and you will receive, that your joy may be full. (John 14:12-14; 16:24)

The fullness of Christian joy is to become what we receive in Christ. Those who are forgiven forgive; those who are loved love; those who receive mercy become merciful. The "greater works" of Christ are worked through those who, though once sinners, become wellsprings of God's grace.

Mary—preserved from sin from her conception—was the first to ask and trust in Jesus' name and cooperate in bringing about the glory of the Father. All of us who are claimed as she is claimed—who trust as she trusts and who ask in the name of Christ as she never ceases to do—take our part in the greater works of God. Not only is this the full joy of Christian discipleship; it is also the full dignity of humanity created and redeemed in Christ.

It would seem, however, as if God does not need our prayers. Christ does everything for those whom he saves, so what is left for us to do?

To assume this is to miss the full measure of what Christ reveals. He makes *our* humanity into the instrument of salvation, into a source of grace.[72] In Christ, God deigns to raise us to the dignity of a cause of his saving work.[73]

The saints have learned this lesson about prayer, and they show us what it means to allow God to make our prayers into instruments of his saving grace. When she was a child, Thérèse of Lisieux was troubled by the biggest news story sweeping across France: that of the convicted murderer Henri Pranzini. Scheduled to be executed for a brutal triple homicide, Pranzini was completely impenitent and even smug in the face of the evil he had almost certainly done.

In this man she would never meet, Thérèse saw a twin tragedy: the tragedy of inhumane violence and the tragedy of a heart hardened against contrition. Thérèse hastened to take this man into her prayer, asking that he become contrite and open himself to God's mercy. As Thérèse readily admitted, she had no power of her own to help this man, especially since she was just a young child living in a small town a hundred miles from Paris. This did not stop her from offering everything she could for Pranzini, which was everything she herself had received from God: "the infinite mercies of Our Lord, the treasures of the Church, and finally . . . a Mass offered for my intentions."[74]

When the newspaper reported that, prior to his execution, Pranzini kissed a crucifix, Thérèse saw the sign of his contrition and the answer to her prayer. For the rest of her life, she would refer to Pranzini as "my first child." God thus blessed both Pranzini and Thérèse: he moved Pranzini to become contrite in his heart and touch his lips to the source of mercy; and he showed Thérèse that he heard her prayers.

No, God need not be informed about what we or others need, as if God does not know. No, we are not cajoling God through our prayers to do something other than what he wills. And no, it is not as if God must be asked first in order to act for our well-being. Rather the possibility of prayer is part of God's gift to us in Christ.

Saints bless sinners with prayers for their well-being, and God blesses his saints by making their prayers matter. By praying for our own and others' needs, God draws us into his work, allowing us to participate in the coming of his kingdom and to align ourselves with the providence of his holy will.[75] God dignifies us in Christ by allowing us to pray: he makes our prayers matter. Both what we need and what we ask matter to God, who receives our prayers in the gift of his Son.[76]

The disciples of Christ receive both the gift of prayer and the responsibility to pray. The responsibility is that *we* ask. In the depths of our infirmities, in the face of the suffering of others, in the events and seasons that seem to offer no clarity or hints as to what God's will might be, we will often not know what we are to pray for. Nevertheless, the responsibility of the disciple is to pray, to offer petitions to the Father in Christ.

The responsibility to pray is founded on and redounds to the gift of Christ to his disciples. First, he allows us to contemplate him in prayer. Second, he teaches us his prayer. And third, he gives us his Spirit, to intercede for us when we do not know how to pray (see Romans 8:26-27). The Spirit does not pray in our place; rather, as St. Thomas Aquinas declares, "the Holy Spirit *makes us ask*, inasmuch as he causes right desires in us . . . aris[ing] from the ardor of love, which he produces in us."[77]

In the Lord's Prayer, Christ forms his disciples in the dispositions of his prayer and teaches us what to desire and in what order to desire things. When clarity is lacking and the boldness for prayer seems to lag, the responsibility of the disciple is to ask again that Christ might teach us how to pray and what to pray for, then wait upon his Spirit, who makes it possible for us to pray. Waiting happens on God's time, not ours.

When disciples do not know what to ask of God, the duty is to ask God to breathe his Spirit into us, so we might discover what we are to ask for and then have the courage to do it. God reveals our deepest desires to us in Christ through the Spirit, so that we might ask God to fulfill those desires.

Our Father in heaven knows what we need and what we desire before we ask (see Matthew 6:8, 32). But like a good father, he allows us to form and make our petitions known to him. We know that when a child is frustrated or troubled by something, a parent could try to solve the problem and quickly take away the trouble. It is the patient and diligent parent who will wait for and even require the child to identify, clarify, and articulate what her issue is. This is how the parent empowers the child.

Just so, the desires that disciples want God to fulfill often precede the petitions offered in prayer. God allows his children to form and make their petitions to him, so that we may become strong in faith and mature in trust, learning to see what matters and then do something about it. We can pray in the name of Christ.[78]

Mary did this skillfully and gracefully at the wedding at Cana. She perceived the need. She offered her petition in response to the need. She waited upon the action of her Son, who manifested the glory of God. Christ awaited her prayer and hastened to act upon it. He exalted her who humbled herself in laying her petition before him.

The Lord knew the wine had run out, as he would know that the centurion's daughter was sick (Matthew 8:5-13), the blind men were blind (Matthew 9:27-30), the man beside the healing pool was sick and had no one to help him (John 5:5-8), and Lazarus would die (John 11:14). But he waited to be asked to fill and to heal and to raise from the dead. He made the petitions of those who asked him for mercy matter, allowing those who asked him to become agents of the salvation he worked.

Completing the Sufferings of Christ

"Now I rejoice in my sufferings for your sake, and in my flesh I complete what is lacking in Christ's afflictions for the sake of his body, that is, the Church" (Colossians 1:24).

You cannot always determine whether someone else suffers, but you can always decide whether someone suffers alone. To share in someone's suffering, to make room in yourself for their needs, to go toward someone to make them the center of your attention in prayer, is in fact to *do something* in the face of evil. The greatest danger evil poses is to disempower us, dragging us into hopelessness and making us despair. To pray is to resist the allure of evil and thus be delivered from it. Prayer leads to joy, because it makes us one with God and unites us to each other in Christ.

Praying for what we or others lack is a form of suffering. It is to confront the good and the fulfillment that we seek by acknowledging its absence. But this confrontation and acknowledgment are not done alone: the one who prays makes her needs known to God. Even when there are no other ways and nothing else is possible, prayer makes a way out of no way and makes possible what is otherwise impossible. In the midst of every kind of powerlessness, praying is an act of courage and determination. Prayer is power.

What is lacking in Christ's afflictions are the needs and petitions that we might claim as our own. Christ does not need our help in making these needs and petitions acceptable to God. What he needs is for us to make these prayers our own, because he will not wrest them from us by force.[79] The glory of God is given in Christ, who makes us fully alive rather than passive puppets. God is glorified when "my flesh" becomes a site for the work of salvation.

When we pray, we undergo a change of heart. The repeated practice of prayer makes us more spacious, creating room to welcome within us not only God but also others.[80] Perhaps the greatest fruit of prayer is that it transforms the one who prays, refashioning the heart into an image of the Father's heart, for God has room for all of us in his heart.

One who knew this well was St. Paul. He once devoted all his time, energy, and passion to tearing down and ruining the lives of Christians. Then, through the grace of Christ and his own practice of the Christian life, he became a source of goodness for those he once persecuted. In his letter to the church at Philippi, Paul reveals as much to his brothers and sisters in Christ:

> I give thanks to my God at every remembrance of you, praying always with joy in my every prayer for all of you, because of your partnership for the gospel from the first day until now. . . . It is right that I should think this way about all of you, because I hold you in my heart, you who are all partners with me in grace. . . . For God is my witness, how I long for all of you with the affection of Christ Jesus. And this is my prayer: that your love may increase ever more. (Philippians 1:3-5, 7-9, NABRE)

Saul of Tarsus had no room in his heart; it was filled to the brim with anger. Paul the disciple, however, practiced making room in his heart for the needs of others. In his own heart, he sought *their* good, *their* joy.[81] There is no end to just how astounding his transformation was. The very man who ardently persecuted these disciples—employing his passion and strength, his time and skill, his knowledge and cunning—came to suffer for them in his heart. It hurts to will the good of others. He made himself dependent on their well-being. He made his heart into a home—a place for others to dwell.[82]

There is no love without suffering. To love means to long and to thirst and to pine for what is good *for someone else*. It is to make yourself a servant of someone else's well-being.

What about those who have no choice but to suffer—those for whom suffering is not taken up freely but rather is impressed upon us without our consent? The first and most common prayer for those who bear such afflictions is to beg for healing, comfort, and solace. Yet healing is not always granted, comfort may not readily be found, and solace can be hard to come by. What then? How ought we to pray? Where is the power in this powerlessness?

The answer is plain, and the reality is hard: addressing your affliction to God makes your suffering into a prayer. Christ holds in his glorified flesh all humanity, not just those who are at ease and comfortable. In fact, those who suffer are especially close to the heart of God. Beginning with Abel, who bore the burden of injustice, the cry of the afflicted is heard by God (see Genesis 4:10). The prayer of the one who suffers unjustly, the one who suffers infirmity, and the one who suffers unshakeable heartache is to direct that suffering to God. It is to say, "I suffer, Lord: hear me!"

That is the first and most important prayer offered by one who suffers. But the witness of God's holy ones shows us even more, if we dare to look with them at the meaning they find in their suffering. They show us how their suffering may even become a petition for someone else's good.

Such is the witness of Robyn Greco, who has suffered both from chronic illness and from a desire to share in the work of Mother Teresa of Calcutta's Missionaries of Charity. In her wisdom, St. Teresa developed a branch of her religious community for those who desired to serve the poorest of the poor but who, because of their own illnesses and limitations, were unable to be active members of the community. St. Teresa invited another form of active participation, by which "sick and suffering" members could offer their limitations for the glory of God.

Here is Robyn Greco's testimony of how her afflictions took on new meaning when made into a prayer offering:

The responsibility and vow of a Sick and Suffering Co-Worker of the Missionaries of Charity is to pray and offer one's sickness and daily suffering to the Lord for the good of one specific Missionary of Charity anywhere in the world. Each Sick and Suffering Co-Worker is assigned a sister somewhere in the world and, in turn, that specific sister will pray daily for her Sick and Suffering Co-Worker. Mother Teresa always called her own personal Sick and Suffering Co-Worker "her other self" because she believed that these people were just as important to the Work (and as much a part of the Missionaries of Charity) as are the professed sisters. She relied heavily on the prayers of her "other self," as [that reliance] allowed those too ill to become a professed Missionary of Charity the ability to share in the Work and, as Mother would say, "Do something beautiful for God."

I have been ill with a disease called Lyme Disease for almost twenty years. I struggle daily with the inability to swallow most solid foods and experience pain (sometimes severe) in all parts of my body, as well as migraine headaches. I have prayed through the years for the Lord to heal me, but thus far a healing has not come. It took me quite some time, but in the last few years (through the mercy of our Lord), I have come to accept God's Will for my life. I feel, through lots and lots of prayer, that God is asking me to be patient and to continue in my suffering. I know that will sound insane to some, but I believe and know that God uses all human suffering for good. I accept His Will and know that, although I may not know or understand how the Lord is using my suffering, someone is receiving grace because of it. . . .

. . . [B]ecoming a Sick and Suffering Co-Worker is the most important thing that has ever happened to me in my forty-two years. There have been many good things that have happened in my years but nothing comes even close to the joy and peace I feel because of this most abundant, pure blessing that God has given to me.

God has given me tangible proof that my years of sufferings have not gone unnoticed by Him, that He has been with me all the time and will continue to be. He is allowing me to use my suffering for something I have longed to be part of, but had no way of making possible. In His mercy and love, the Father has granted me the privilege to share in the suffering of his Son, our Lord Jesus, on the Cross. By willingly uniting my suffering with Christ's, I can STILL be happy and peaceful through my pain and sickness. I will still pray and ask for a healing, but my new vocation as a Sick and Suffering Co-Worker of the Missionaries of Charity sustains me. If a physical healing never comes, I am already healed in ways that the world will never understand.[83]

In his mercy, the Lord makes suffering meaningful. How? First by taking on our suffering as his own, and then by giving us the grace to offer our suffering as a gift through him. Mother Teresa knew this secret of grace and so created this way of participation in the work of her Missionaries. She trusted that what Christ promises is true: through him all things are possible. In Robyn's case, that meant being mystically united to an "other self" who served the "unwanted, unclaimed, and unloved." Robyn's suffering became a petition for the well-being of many in the Body of Christ.[84]

The sufferings of Christ are completed in his disciples who allow their sufferings to become sources of communion. St. Paul stretches his heart to make room for many others. Robyn Greco offers her afflictions for the good of the least among us and the missionaries who serve them. Both allow their humanity to be drawn into the mystery of Christ, who by the mystery of his incarnation through to his ascension unites our humanity everlastingly to his Father in love. The glory of God is made manifest in those who suffer to love in prayer, sharing in the salvific work of our one and only Savior.

Discovering Ourselves in the Words of Jesus

When you have lifted up the Son of man, then you will know that I am he, and that I do nothing on my own authority but speak thus as the Father taught me. And he who sent me is with me; he has not left me alone, for I always do what is pleasing to him. . . .

. . . If you continue in my word, you are truly my disciples, and you will know the truth, and the truth will make you free. . . .

. . . Truly, truly, I say to you, if any one keeps my word, he will never see death. (John 8:28-29, 31-32, 51).

Jesus is never alone; the Father is always with him. In giving himself to his disciples, Jesus gives not just himself but also the Father. The communion of the Spirit that lives between the Father and the Son becomes the communion that unites Jesus' disciples to God. This communion is expressed in terms of hearing and speaking: the Son welcomes the word and the will of the Father, then acts according to what he hears. For those who will be his disciples, what matters is receiving what Jesus speaks and does, then acting accordingly.

This life of communion is glimpsed in St. Paul, who received Christ, allowed himself to be gathered into the Father's heart through Christ, and thereby opened his heart to do what the Father does: he gathered others into his own heart, so that their "love may abound more and more" (Philippians 1:9). Robyn Greco practices giving herself to her Missionary of Charity and, through that missionary, to the poorest of the poor. She does this in response to Christ's sharing in her suffering and enabling her to offer what she suffers as a sacrifice to the Father. Christ is the one in whom God and humanity meet, and that meeting takes the form of sharing words: hearing and speaking as one.

When in chapter 2 we contemplated Jesus as the Son of Man, in his descent to take on the words of the psalmist as his own prayer, we recalled that every dimension of the human condition is made present in the psalms. Praying the words of the psalmist as his own was part of Jesus' taking on the fullness of the human condition, from the loftiest exclamation of praise to the last doleful lament. Thus Jesus opened his heart to those whose lives resonate in these words. He took on their condition as his condition. He does that still, thereby uniting those whose condition he shares to the Father, who is always with the Son.

When Jesus says, "Continue in my word," he means that we are to do what he does. He allows the words of others to become his words: he shares in their condition by praying their prayers as his own. For those who follow Jesus, the gift and the task are to join in his prayer, which means allowing the prayers of others to become our own. Every Christian prayer is an exercise of communion—an exercise in being drawn into the communion of the Father and the Son and of allowing our needs and desires to be united to the needs and desires of our brothers and sisters.

"Prayer is the capacity to inhabit someone else's suffering," writes Timothy Verdon.[85] For the Christian, this means two things at once.

On the one hand, it means that, through prayer, we offer our sufferings as a plea to Christ, who makes them known to the Father. In the exchange of prayer, our sufferings are joined to his as one offering to the Father.

On the other hand, through prayer we open ourselves to allowing the suffering of others to find a home in us. We practice bearing their pleas and petitions as if they were our own—in a word, we become our brother's and our sister's keeper. In fact, these pleas and petitions *do* become our own. The heart of the Christian at prayer becomes an altar on which God's communion is prepared.

"As meeting place of God's desire and human hunger, the praying heart shares the expectation of the poor and the super-abundant gifts of the Father," declares Jean Corbon, marveling at the mysterious exchange in Christ that prayer makes possible. "The praying heart is present at the banquet table of love, less in the festivity of the eucharistic meal than in the painful hope of those who do not yet share in it."[86]

As Christ sought not his own private good but rather the good of others in obedience to his Father's will, so too does the Christian at prayer continually seek the sacrifice of letting go of private concerns and selfish desires in order to will the good of others as if it were his or her own good. This, in fact, is what the saints never cease doing. In their prayer for the good of others and for all the Church, the saints prepare for the final heavenly banquet. Every Christian who makes their heart available to God and the needs of others in prayer joins the saints in this longing and preparation.

Christian prayer is sharing in the work and the life of Christ, in whom and with whom the Father is at work and alive. A disciple never prays alone: he prays in and with Christ, even as he prays to Christ, who is united with the Father. In so doing, the disciple opens himself to sharing in what Christ himself suffers out of love: the desire for the well-being of others.

How does a disciple learn to speak the words of Christ and allow Christ to speak the disciple's words? First by praying the prayer that Jesus gave to his disciples—the Lord's Prayer— and then by praying the words that Jesus prayed, the psalms. To not just read the psalms but indeed to *pray* the psalms is to join in the words Jesus addresses to his Father.[87]

Travis Lacy grasped the significance and tremendous beauty of praying the psalms during an immersion experience at a Cistercian monastery, where the monks dedicate themselves to praying all 150 psalms each week, according to the Liturgy of the Hours:

> The point is this: praying the Psalms, inhaling and exhaling their cries, making their words our own, and suffusing our sighs with its laments, entails an unavoidably and painfully direct encounter with the human condition. Not merely to read, but to *pray* the words, "ten thousand enemies may fall at my right" (Ps. 91:7), or "my one companion is darkness" (Ps. 88:18), requires a confrontation with the infinitude of our temptations and the depths of our anxieties. Perhaps this is the necessary, systolic, preface to the diastole of praise that constitutes much of the Psalter. If declarations of the Lord's steadfast love (Ps. 136) ring hollow, and if repeated exhortations to praise (Ps. 148) are sterile, perhaps we do not know the reasons we have been given to sing. But Psalmody provides these reasons, if only we (or at least, I) would not run from them. To be human is to be often alone, often dejected, often beset by temptation, but the psalms make this sadness the substance of our worship. Thus the work of glorification requires courage, and it cannot be cheaply gained.[88]

The truth that sets us free is Jesus Christ, who gathers the needs of others as his own while he offers himself to the Father. True freedom is not only being claimed by him but also sharing in his offering. It is the freedom of moving outside the confines of our own private or individual concerns and becoming open to the needs of others, especially those of the least among us. This is the freedom of Christ, who prays to his Father "that they may all be one" (John 17:21).

Disciples who pray for the sake of and in communion with others are the fruit of Jesus' prayer. We come to abide in his word and "will never see death" (John 8:51).

Sign of the Promise

> Truly, truly, I say to you, the hour is coming, and now is, when the dead will hear the voice of the Son of God, and those who hear will live. For as the Father has life in himself, so he has granted the Son also to have life in himself, and has given him authority to execute judgment, because he is the Son of man. Do not marvel at this; for the hour is coming when all who are in the tombs will hear his voice and come forth, those who have done good, to the resurrection of life, and those who have done evil, to the resurrection of judgment. (John 5:25-29)

Lazarus died. He was dead four days. His body was like the void and darkness before the Lord's word of creation "in the beginning" (Genesis 1:1-2). As soon as Christ spoke into the tomb, Lazarus received again the gift of life. He who heard lived.

Lazarus is the last sign of the "hour [that] is coming." At that hour, the full glory of God will be revealed in Christ, in whom the life of God becomes the life of humanity. Lazarus died again, but in time the Lord's voice will give life to all who hear him, and that life will never end.

Mother Mary was the privileged witness to the full measure of Jesus' first sign. Like others present at the wedding at Cana, she witnessed the power of Jesus' word to turn water into wine. But beyond what others experienced, she witnessed the power of her own petition being heard and heeded by Jesus.

In this last sign, who is the privileged witness? Certainly many knew that Lazarus was dead and then saw him alive again. All of them were witnesses. Then there were Mary and Martha, who wept bitterly over their brother's death and were thus witnesses in another way: their gravest sorrow turned to indescribable joy. They also witnessed Jesus' sharing in their sorrow—"Jesus wept" (John 11:35)—before responding to it.

And yet is it not Lazarus who witnessed what no one else did? Lazarus was the one who felt the word of the Lord enter into his dead flesh and give life. He alone walked toward Jesus in obedience to his command, and each of those steps was powered by the word that called him back from death. In his very body, Lazarus heard the word of God and acted on it. He is a sign of the power of the Lord's word.

From where though does Christ's word come? When he speaks, whose voice is heard? With his voice he says that he does not speak on his own but that "the Father who sent me has himself given me commandment what to say and what to speak" (John 12:49). Jesus is the Father's Word, and he speaks in communion with the Father.

Jesus is also the one who humbled himself before the words of his mother. The voice that Lazarus heard was alive with the love of the Father in union with the love of the Blessed Mother. It was a human voice that brought life to Lazarus again, a human voice that was the sign and instrument of the divine Word.

Walking out of the tomb, Lazarus was a man beginning to pray. He heard and acted on the word of the Lord. The Lord's voice echoed in his body, while each of his movements—from the silent beat of his heart to each new footfall—testified to the one who called him.

Lazarus was not the fulfillment of the promise but only its sign. He was still a man mired in sin, inclined to cease listening to the voice who gave him life, sluggish in welcoming and responding to the word the Lord spoke to him. He was still bound for the grave, even though he was rescued from it for some amount of time.

In prayer, though, every time Lazarus would heed the word of the Lord, welcome that word into his heart, and speak that word, he would glimpse and long for his own fulfillment in the communion of God, where he would never fail to hear the Lord's word and live. His revived flesh reveals that even from the point of death, the word of God may be received, be responded to, and generate life. Even wrapped in burial cloths, the one whom the Lord loves may allow the Lord to share his burdens and also receive the mission to share in the joy and sorrow of those whom the Lord claims as his own.

The voice that Lazarus heard and received was begotten of the Father before the foundation of the world. This is the same voice that was fashioned through the psalms to resound with the whole human condition. In the tomb Lazarus heard this word of life and responded. In the days and years that followed, his task was to learn how to take on that word as his own, offering himself into the communion of God with all those claimed in Christ.

A Share in Glory

"Behold, I am the handmaid of the Lord; let it be to me according to your word" (Luke 1:38). Bolder or more beautiful words no creature like us has ever spoken. The young maid from Nazareth pledges herself in obedience to the Word of God. She promises to receive, to listen, and to follow. She says, "I do," and, "I will," in the same breath, uttering a yes to God that gathers up who she has been and offers all she will be.

The Word of God whom she welcomes will surprise her over and over again, and she will struggle to continually heed the Word whom she receives in her body and ponders in her heart. Yet she never doubts; she trusts. "With all the strength she can muster she listens to this Word as it grows more and more vast . . . ; its dimensions almost tear her asunder, yet it is for this, for everything, that she gave her consent right at the start."[89]

Yes, from the start she consented to receiving the gift of this divine Word, who became flesh and dwelt among us, beginning with her. And in the end, she consents to dwelling in God, who came to dwell in her.

The glorious assumption of the Most Blessed Virgin Mary is the fulfillment of the sign of the raising of Lazarus. She hears the Word always and follows into glory everlasting. She is God's creation perfected in prayer.

Mary's entire body becomes a prayer in Christ. She received him fully, and in the end, she is lifted up fully in him to the Father. She is the mystery of the boldness and beauty of the children of God.

In his Gospel, the beloved disciple recounts only two occasions of Jesus' speaking to his mother. The first is at the wedding at Cana in Galilee, when in response to her petition he says, "O woman, what have you do to with me?" (John 2:4). The second is while he hangs on the cross, and looking down at Mary and the beloved disciple, he says, "Woman, behold, your son!" (John 19:26). The first of these words comes before his first sign, and the other at the completion of his sacrifice.

The pain and fidelity of heeding the Word of God, whom Mary welcomed at the annunciation, are laid bare here. In Cana she exercised the trust to lay her petition into her Son's hands and yet consented again to follow where he led: "Do whatever he tells you" (John 2:5). On Calvary she follows his will even to the point of letting him go and accepting the one he gives her to care for: this beloved disciple, who stands in place of all those whom her Son claims as his own with his Father's love. In the first movement, she offered the needs of others to her Son. In the last movement, she accepts the responsibility her Son gives her to care for the needs of those he loves. Through her love of Christ, all disciples are her children.

What became of this woman's heart? If we could peer inside, what would we see? Would we not see the face of her Son, who is the Word she pondered to the end? And would we not see all the others whose needs she receives and offers to her Son, as though those needs were the needs of her own child? Would not our own faces be freshly imprinted upon her heart?

The assumption of Mary is the completion of the annunciation, just as Christ's ascension is the completion of the incarnation. Mary followed Jesus in rising to the same degree in which she received him in his descending—that is, completely, with all her being. He assumed our humanity in her, and her humanity was assumed into glory with him. Christ never lets go of the humanity he takes on—he never lets go of her. In prayer she allows this union to be made complete: saying yes to the God who says yes to her. She is crowned Queen of Heaven and Earth.

That same beloved disciple whom Mary received as her own child told his community, "We are God's children now; it does not yet appear what we shall be, but we know that when he appears we shall be like him, for we shall see him as he is" (1 John 3:2). In the glorious assumption of her who loved that disciple as her own child and whom that disciple loved as his mother, the mystery of what we shall be is revealed. We shall be one in the prayer of Christ, our words mingling as one, our flesh radiant with the glory of God, dwelling in God, who desires that we "may all be one" (John 17:21).

As first with Mary, so with all who become beloved disciples in her care, heeding whom she heeded and following whom she followed. The prayer of Mary's Son is our salvation, and all who pray into him receive him who shares everything with us. From his Blessed Mother to the last of the disciples, Christ hears everything we offer him in prayer and draws all into the heart of the Father.

For Reflection

1. Have you ever thought of yourself as an agent or instrument of someone's salvation? In what specific ways do you live out this bold statement in your prayer for others and in attention to their needs?

2. Do you allow yourself to be drawn into the suffering of others? How do you support those who are suffering while maintaining your own sense of the goodness of the Lord?

3. The psalms cover the entire range of human experience, from despair and lamentation to joy and confident trust. How do you incorporate the psalms into your daily prayer? How can you let these prayers that Jesus prayed bring you closer to the Father?

The Time
for Prayer

"I will arise and go to my father" (Luke 15:18).

The prodigal son had nothing left; he had lost it all. His inheritance was gone. His prospects had evaporated. His honor was in tatters. And yet he was still his father's son, disfigured as he was. He still belonged at home, distant as he had become. He still hoped, bleak as his condition was. So from that "far country . . . he arose and came to his father" (Luke 15:13, 20).

When Jesus told that parable to the tax collectors and sinners, and within earshot of the Pharisees and scribes (Luke 15:1-2), he revealed who he is. He is the one who makes it possible to seek the Father from wherever we find ourselves, even when bitter of heart or mired in the filth of sin. He is the one who gives that lost son the inspiration of prayer—that desire to rise and go to the Father. He is the one who descends to our condition and from there addresses his Father. He is the one in whom that lost son begins to move.

The love of Christ reaches that son who has lost everything. Because the only-begotten Son of the Father descended to that sad and lonely place, the lost son may begin to pray from that "far country." His sin, his sorrow, and his desperation may become offerings of prayer, because Christ makes that lonely place holy by his presence.

Jesus does not forget the Pharisees and scribes who over-hear him. To those bitter ones, he presents the elder son—the son who is always near home, ever dutiful, and oh so pleased with himself. The Pharisees' and scribes' murmuring over Jesus' feasting with the tax collectors and sinners reverberates in the anger and disdain the elder son has over his father's feast for the younger son (Luke 15:28-29).

Jesus does not just chide the Pharisees and scribes though; he also beckons them. He allows them to hear the father say to the elder brother, "Son, you are always with me, and all that is mine is yours" (15:31). Through Jesus the embittered can rediscover themselves as the beloved of the Father.

The younger son and the elder son are both meant to be at home in their father's house. The tax collectors and sinners, the Pharisees and scribes, hear that together. Jesus is the one who reveals this to them. It is indeed his prayer.

"In my Father's house are many rooms; if it were not so, would I have told you that I go to prepare a place for you?" (John 14:2). The true home for all whom Christ claims as his own is his Father's house. He came from his Father to share in all that we have and all that we are, taking on our flesh as his own. From where we are, the Son of God himself said, "I will arise and go to my Father's house."

Prayer is receiving him who comes to us and rising with him who takes us home. Every prayer offered in his name is a step toward home. All can be offered through him in prayer.

Christ gives us himself to contemplate, he teaches us how to pray, and he hears our prayers. But as his disciples, we have the responsibility to make his prayer our own. Shall we pray?

"Behold, now is the acceptable time; behold, now is the day of salvation" (2 Corinthians 6:2).

Notes

1. Joseph Ratzinger, *The God of Jesus Christ: Meditations on the Triune God*, trans. Brian McNeil, 2nd ed. (San Francisco: Ignatius Press, 2018), 82.
2. For a wonderful reflection on the priority of love in relation to the theology of St. Thomas Aquinas and St. Bonaventure, see Benedict XVI, "Love Sees Further than Reason," *EWTN*, March 17, 2010, https://www.ewtn.com/catholicism/library/st-bonaventure--st-thomas-aquinas-6263.
3. Note that the verse numbers in different translations of the Book of Psalms do not always align. For example, I am using the RSVCE translation throughout most of this book, and in that translation, "The LORD is near to the brokenhearted" is Psalm 34:18, while the equivalent NABRE translation, "The LORD is close to the brokenhearted," is 34:19. The NABRE often counts the explanatory note about the psalm—"A Psalm of David, . . ." in this case—as the first verse, while the RSVCE does not. You may find in other translations differences

in the numbering of a psalm itself; for example, Psalm 34 is Psalm 33 in some Bibles. This is due to different numbering systems in the ancient Hebrew Masoretic text and the Greek Septuagint (and later Latin Vulgate). Guides to different numbering systems are available online and elsewhere (with helpful charts often provided). As a general rule of thumb, if you search for a verse in a psalm but do not find what you expected, check one verse ahead and one verse behind, as well as one psalm ahead and one psalm behind.

4. For a scholarly essay on the permanence of Christ's humanity, see Karl Rahner, "The Eternal Significance of the Humanity of Jesus for Our Relationship with God," in *Theological Investigations*, trans. Cornelius Ernst et al., vol. 3 (Limerick, Ireland: Mary Immaculate College, 2000), 35–46.

5. Hans Urs von Balthasar, *Prayer*, trans. Graham Harrison (San Francisco: Ignatius Press, 1986), 9.

6. I am indebted to Hans Urs von Balthasar for bringing me to this insight. See von Balthasar, 83–84. The Catholic media scholar Marshall McLuhan did much to develop critical reflection on the importance of media in relation to the message that is conveyed, even going so far as to proclaim that "the medium is the message." Among his many illuminating essays and books, one extensive introduction to his thought is Marshall McLuhan, *Understanding Media: The Extensions of Man*, ed. W. Terrence Gordon, critical ed. (Corte Madera, CA: Gingko Press, 2003).

7. Hans Urs von Balthasar, as quoted in Ratzinger, *The God of Jesus Christ*, 84–85.

8. Kristin M. Collier, "The Theobiology of a Mother's Voice," March 3, 2020, *Church Life Journal*, https://churchlifejournal.nd.edu/articles/a-relational -theology-of-biology/.

9. Collier.

10. Kristin M. Collier, "Some Human Beings Carry Remnants of Other Humans in Their Bodies," *Church Life Journal*, July 25, 2019, https://churchlifejournal.nd.edu/ articles/human-beings-carry-remnants-of-other-humans -in-their-bodies/.

11. Collier.

12. Collier.

13. Collier.

14. Ratzinger, *The God of Jesus Christ*, 80.

15. Lin-Manuel Miranda and Jeremy McCarter, *Hamilton: The Revolution*, illustrated ed. (New York: Grand Central Publishing, 2016), 128–30.

16. Melito of Sardis writes, "He descended from Heaven to earth for suffering humankind; he clothed himself in our human nature in the Virgin's womb and was born as man, assuming the sufferings of suffering mankind through a body subject to suffering" (Homily on Easter, 65–67; cf. Hebrews 10:5-10), quoted in Timothy Verdon, *Art & Prayer: The Beauty of Turning to God* (Brewster, MA: Mount Tabor, 2016), 63.

17. The Catholic theologian Romano Guardini leads his readers into the Garden of Gethsemane by way of a sobering and weighty self-examination and indeed a confession of one's sin. See Romano Guardini, *The Lord*, trans. Elinor Briefs (Washington, DC: Regnery Publishing Company, 2013), 447.

18. Verdon, *Art & Prayer: The Beauty of Turning to God*, 9.

19. A profound and severely under-read meditation on the depth of Jesus' handing over of himself is presented throughout W. H. Vanstone's *The Stature of Waiting* (London: Darton, Longman and Todd, 2001).

20. For a stunning sermon on the temptation and suffering of the Son of God, see John Henry Newman, "The Humiliation of the Eternal Son," in *Parochial and Plain Sermons* (San Francisco: Ignatius, 1997), 583–93.

21. Mother Teresa, Brian Kolodiejchuk, *Mother Teresa: Come Be My Light: The Private Writings of the Saint of Calcutta* (New York, NY: Crown Publishing Group, 2007), 232.

22. For a scholarly analysis of the controversies surrounding this line's status in the canon and its history of interpretation, see Nathan Eubank, "A Disconcerting Prayer: On the Originality of Luke 23:34a," *Journal of Biblical Literature* 129, no. 3 (2010): 521–36.

23. For more on the distinction and relationship between forgiveness and reconciliation, see Leonard J. DeLorenzo, "Only Reconciliation Can Cancel Transgressions," *Church Life Journal*, August 6, 2020, https://churchlifejournal.nd.edu/articles/only-reconciliation-can-cancel-transgressions/.

24. These four women are Sr. Dorothy Kazel, OSU, Sr. Ita Ford, MM, Sr. Maura Clarke, MM, and lay missionary Jean Donovan. For more, see Stephanie M. Huezo, "The Murdered Churchwomen in El Salvador," December 2020, https://origins.osu.edu/milestones/ murdered-churchwomen-el-salvador.

25. See Gregory Boyle, *Tattoos on the Heart: The Power of Boundless Compassion* (New York: Free Press, 2010).

26. St. Augustine, as quoted in Laurence Kriegshauser, *Praying the Psalms in Christ* (Notre Dame, IN: University of Notre Dame Press, 2009), 4; see Augustine, "Exposition on Psalm 86," 1, *New Advent*, https:// www.newadvent.org/fathers/1801086.htm.

27. Hans Urs von Balthasar, *Mysterium Paschale: The Mystery of Easter*, trans. Aidan Nichols (San Francisco: Ignatius Press, 2000), 163; see Joseph Ratzinger, *Eschatology: Death and Eternal Life*, ed. Aidan Nichols, trans. Michael Waldstein, 2nd ed. (Washington, DC: Catholic University of America Press, 2007), 93.

28. St. Gregory of Nazianzus most memorably expressed this truth of faith, which has echoed through the ages (see Epistle 101, 32: SC 208, 50). For a beautiful and illuminating homily dealing with the teaching of Gregory, see Benedict XVI, "General Audience of 22 August 2007: Saint Gregory Nazianzus (2)," http://www .vatican.va/content/benedict-xvi/en/audiences/2007/ documents/hf_ben-xvi_aud_20070822.html.

29. To read this whole "back story," see Julie Zauzmer, "The World Saw Pope Francis Bless a Boy with Cerebral Palsy. Here's What We Didn't See," *Washington Post*, October 12, 2015, sec. Local, https://www.washingtonpost.com/local/the-world-saw-pope-francis-bless-a-boy-with-cerebral-palsy-heres-what-we-didnt-see/2015/10/11/9d312e96-6c78-11e5-b31c-d80d62b53e28_story.html.

30. This, in brief, is the response of Alexander of Alexandria, then the Council of Nicaea, and most pointedly Athanasius to the heretical view of Christ espoused by the Arians.

31. Irenaeus of Lyons, *Against Heresies*, ed. Alexander Roberts, James Donaldson, and Arthur Cleveland Coxe (n.p.: Ex Fontibus Company, 2012), III.XIX (332-35).

32. *Orationes* 1, 5: SC 247, 78; quoted in Benedict XVI, "General Audience of 22 August 2007: Saint Gregory Nazianzus (2)."

33. Pope Francis accounted for himself in precisely this way during the first major interview of his pontificate, while speaking explicitly of Caravaggio's painting. See Pope Francis and Antonio Spadaro, SJ, "A Big Heart Open to God," *America Magazine*, September 30, 2013, http://americamagazine.org/pope-interview. See also Leonard J. DeLorenzo, *Witness: Learning to Tell the Stories of Grace That Illumine Our Lives* (Notre Dame, IN: Ave Maria, 2016), 1–6.

34. St. Augustine develops this complex thought in *The Trinity*, ed. John Rotelle, trans. Edmund Hill (Hyde Park, NY: New City Press, 2012), especially I.8.16–19; cf. Khaled Anatolios, *Retrieving Nicaea: The Development and Meaning of Trinitarian Doctrine* (Grand Rapids, MI: Baker Academic, 2011), 247–49.

35. See Exodus 3:14; cf. John 8:58; 18:5, 6.

36. See Job 38:8; Psalm 65:7; 89:9; 107:29.

37. See Psalm 105:4; 1 Chronicles 16:11. For a marvelous meditation on Mary's pondering heart, see Colleen Halpin, "The Pondering Heart: Notre Dame's Special Consecration to Our Lady," *Church Life Journal*, October 7, 2017, https://churchlifejournal.nd.edu/articles/the-pondering-heart-notre-dames-special-consecration-to-our-lady/; as well as Ann W. Astell, "Mary's Pondering Heart and the Idea of a Catholic University," in *I Call You Friends: John Cavadini and the Vision of Catholic Leadership for Higher Education*, ed. Leonard J. DeLorenzo and Timothy P. O'Malley (Eugene, OR: Pickwick, 2019), 22–35.

38. See John 21:6-7, 15-19.

39. This particular section on the agony in the garden draws in part from my reflection in *A God Who Questions* (Huntington, IN: Our Sunday Visitor, 2019), 87–92.

40. This brilliant and beautiful articulation of the "quiescence" of the humanity and divinity of Jesus in alternating turns comes from Irenaeus of Lyons, *Against Heresies*, 334 [III.XIX.3].

41. Simon Gershon, as quoted in Patricia Treece, *A Man for Others: Maximilian Kolbe the "Saint of Auschwitz"* (Libertyville, IL: Marytown, 2013), 199–200.

42. See Joseph Ratzinger, *Introduction to Christianity*, 2nd ed. (San Francisco: Ignatius Press, 2004), 313.

43. Jean Corbon, *The Wellspring of Worship*, trans. Matthew O'Connell, 2nd ed. (San Francisco: Ignatius, 2005), 61–62.

44. Paul Türks, *Philip Neri: The Fire of Joy*, trans. Daniel Utrecht (New York: Continuum, 1995), 12–17; cf. Antonio Gallonio, *The Life of St. Philip Neri*, trans. Jerome Bertram (San Francisco: Ignatius, 2005), 17.

45. John Henry Newman, "The Mission of St. Philip Neri, Part 2," *Newman Reader: Sermons Preached on Various Occasions*, Sermon 12, 7, http://www.newman-reader.org/works/occasions/sermon12-2.html. For more on St. Philip Neri, see also Leonard J. DeLorenzo, "It's More Effective to Attract Than to Simply Chastise," *Church Life Journal*, May 29, 2018, https://church-lifejournal.nd.edu/articles/its-more-effective-to-attract-than-to-simply-chastise/.

46. See Augustine, *The Trinity*, I.18. While meditating on another of Christ's mysteries—the finding of Jesus in the Temple at age twelve—Balthasar offers an illuminating comment that resonates with Augustine's insight: "We find him definitively only in the place of the Father, in heaven, which is to say when finding no longer implies containing God within our space, but rather when it means that we have been found by

God, that we have entered into his space, then we are 'known by God' (1 Corinthians 13:12)." (Hans Urs von Balthasar, *The Threefold Garland: The World's Salvation in Mary's Prayer* [San Francisco: Ignatius Press, 1982], 60).

47. See John Paul II, *Catechesi Tradendae*, 1979, no. 5, http://www.vatican.va/content/john-paul-ii/en/apost _exhortations/documents/hf_jp-ii_exh_16101979 _catechesi-tradendae.html.

48. St. Augustine, Epistle 130, 12, 22: PL 33, 503, quoted in *Catechism* 2762.

49. St. Thomas Aquinas, *Summa Theologiae* II-II, 83, 9, quoted in *Catechism* 2763.

50. The full seven petitions are recorded in St. Matthew's Gospel (6:9-13), whereas St. Luke includes a briefer version of the prayer, containing only five petitions (11:2-4).

51. Franz Jägerstätter, *Franz Jägerstätter: Letters and Writings from Prison*, ed. Erna Putz, trans. Robert Krieg (Maryknoll, NY: Orbis Books, 2009), 156.

52. For St. Francis of Assisi's ruminations on the petitions of the Lord's Prayer, see *Francis and Clare: The Complete Works*, trans. Regis J. Armstrong and Ignatius C. Brady, new ed. (New York: Paulist Press, 1986), 104–6.

53. When naming Thérèse of Lisieux a Doctor of the Church, Pope St. John Paul II identified her eminent doctrine as the fundamental conviction that God is our Father and we are his children. This, he says, is at the heart of the gospel (see Pope John Paul II, *Apostolic*

Letter: Divini Amoris Scientia, 1997, http://www
.vatican.va/content/john-paul-ii/en/apost_letters/1997/
documents/hf_jp-ii_apl_19101997_divini-amoris.html.

54. See International Theological Commission, "Some
Current Questions in Eschatology," 1992, 1.2.3, http://
www.vatican.va/roman_curia/congregations/cfaith/
cti_documents/rc_cti_1990_problemi-attuali
-escatologia_en.html.

55. Ratzinger, *The God of Jesus Christ*, 34.

56. Dorothy Day, *By Little and By Little: The Selected
Writings of Dorothy Day*, ed. Robert Ellsberg (New
York: Alfred A. Knopf, 1984), 110.

57. Day, 100.

58. C. S. Lewis presents this means of separation in *The
Great Divorce* (San Francisco: HarperOne, 2000), see
71.

59. Augustine, *The Confessions*, trans. Maria Boulding
(New York: Vintage Books, 1998), 3 (bk. 1, 1).

60. Pieter Hugo and Susan Dominus, "Portraits of Reconciliation," *The New York Times*, April 4, 2014, sec.
Magazine, https://www.nytimes.com/interactive/
2014/04/06/magazine/06-pieter-hugo-rwanda-portraits.
html; cf. DeLorenzo, "Only Reconciliation Can Cancel
Transgressions."

61. John Henry Newman, "Forms of Private Prayer," in
Parochial and Plain Sermons (San Francisco: Ignatius,
1997), 172.

62. These three parables are named "three principal
parables on prayer" in the *Catechism of the Catholic
Church*, 2613.

63. See Klyne Snodgrass, *Stories with Intent: A Comprehensive Guide to the Parables of Jesus* (Grand Rapids, MI: William B. Eerdmans, 2008), 442–45.

64. Snodgrass, 448–49.

65. See Exodus 22:21-24; Deuteronomy 10:18; 24:17; 26:12; 27:19; Isaiah 1:17; Psalms 68:5; 146:9; Jeremiah 22:3; Zechariah 7:10; Malachi 3:5; James 1:27, among many instances in the Old and New Testaments.

66. See Snodgrass, *Stories with Intent*, 466.

67. Flannery O'Connor portrays this Pharisee perfectly in Ruby Turpin, the main character of her short story "Revelation." See Flannery O'Connor, *The Complete Stories*, 1st ed. (New York: Farrar, Straus and Giroux, 1972), 488–510.

68. John Henry Newman, "Rising with Christ," in *Parochial and Plain Sermons*, 1323.

69. Corbon, *The Wellspring of Worship*, 214.

70. For a parallel reflection on this passage, which in part informs the reflection I have written here, in part anticipates it, and in part completes it, see *A God Who Questions*, 67–74.

71. The seven signs are changing water into wine at the wedding at Cana (John 2:1-11), the healing of the royal official's son (John 4:46-54), the healing of the paralytic in Bethesda (John 5:1-15), the feeding of the five thousand (John 6:5-14), walking on water (John 6:16-24), the healing of the man born blind (John 9:1-7), and the raising of Lazarus (John 11:1-45).

72. See Irenaeus of Lyons, *Against Heresies*, III.16-19 (313-35), and especially III.18.7 (331-32).

73. Francesca Murphy brings forth Thomas Aquinas's teaching on this point in "The Trinity and Prayer," in *The Oxford Handbook of the Trinity*, ed. Gilles Emery and Matthew Levering (Oxford: Oxford University Press, 2011), 513–14.

74. Saint Thérèse of Lisieux, *Story of a Soul*, trans. John Clarke (Washington, DC: ICS Publications, 1996), 99.

75. It is well worth thinking about this gift and responsibility of participating in the coming of the kingdom in light of the "preferential option for the poor." For an excellent point of departure for these considerations, see Gustavo Gutiérrez, "Option for the Poor," in *Mysterium Liberationis: Fundamental Concepts of Liberation Theology*, ed. Ignacio Ellacuría and Jon Sobrino (Maryknoll, NY: Orbis, 1993), 239–50.

76. This paragraph presents, in brief, the teaching of St. Thomas Aquinas on the question "Whether it is becoming to pray?" *Summa Theologiae* II–II, q.83, a.2, available at https://www.newadvent.org/summa/3083.htm#article2.

77. St. Thomas Aquinas, "Romans Commentary" (paragraph 693), quoted in Murphy, *The Oxford Handbook of the Trinity*, 508. Emphasis added in Murphy's text. Focusing on the insights from such figures as Thomas Aquinas, Saint Augustine, John Henry Newman, and Hans Urs von Balthasar. It explains Augustine argued that the proper use of contemplation is the worship

of the Triune God, Aquinas believed that petition-
ary prayer is mediated through the predestination of
Christ, von Balthasar held that contemplative prayer
is centered on the humanity of Christ, and Newman's
"real assent" relates to the liturgical appropriation
of individual dogmas of faith. It suggests that prayer
requires the confluence of invocation and meditation,
made possible in various forms by real assent to God
revealing himself in the humanity of Christ as the
mediator/intercessor/propitiator and inspiring us by his
Spirit.

78. This paragraph presents, in brief, the teaching of St.
Thomas Aquinas on the question "Whether prayer is
an act of the appetitive power," in *Summa Theologiae* II-II, q.83, a.1, available at https://www.newadvent.
org/summa/3083.htm#article1.

79. St. Augustine muses on the mystery of this mystical
participation in the sufferings of Christ in "Exposition
on Psalm 86," 5.

80. For more on this, consider St. Thomas Aquinas on
the questions of "Is union an effect of love?" and "Is
mutual indwelling an effect of love" in *Summa Theologiae* I-II, q.28, a.1–2, http://www.newadvent.org/sum-
ma/2028.htm.

81. Pope Francis marvels at the beauty and health of Paul's
heart, which he identifies as the heart of an evangelizer,
in *Evangelii Gaudium: The Joy of the Gospel* (Washington, DC: United States Conference of Catholic
Bishops, 2013), 281–82.

82. This paragraph is taken from my book on forming people for life in the Church, specifically from chapter 4 of part 1. See Leonard J. DeLorenzo, *Turn to the Lord* (Collegeville, MN: Liturgical Press, 2021).

83. This testimonial first appeared on Gary Zimak's blog and is used here with the permission of both Mr. Zimak and Ms. Greco, to whom I owe a debt of gratitude. See Robyn Greco, "Suffering for the Lord," *Following the Truth*, July 19, 2012, https://followingthetruth.com/suffering-for-the-lord/.

84. For further development on some of the themes relating to Mother Teresa and the Missionaries of Charity, see my article "Mother Teresa and the Pain of Joy," *Church Life Journal*, September 1, 2016, https://churchlifejournal.nd.edu/articles/mother-teresa-and-the-pain-of-joy/.

85. Verdon, *Art & Prayer: The Beauty of Turning to God*, 62.

86. Corbon, *The Wellspring of Worship*, 215.

87. On praying in and with Christ in the Psalms, see especially St. Augustine, "Exposition on Psalm 86."

88. Travis Lacy, "You Gotta Confront Who You Are!" *Church Life Journal*, September 18, 2019, https://churchlifejournal.nd.edu/articles/you-gotta-confront-who-you-are/.

89. Balthasar, *Prayer*, 29.